# Mindful Tech

*Sage Yamamoto's Ethical Innovations*

Aisha Schmitt

ISBN: 9783100005530
*Imprint: Telephasic Workshop*
Copyright © 2024 Aisha Schmitt.
All Rights Reserved.

# Contents

**Introduction**    **1**
The Rise of Mindful Tech    1

**Chapter One: A Curious Mind**    **9**
Early Life and Influences    9
The College Years    20

**Chapter Two: Disrupting the Industry**    **33**
Creating an Ethical Tech Startup    33
Innovations that Matter    45

**Bibliography**    **53**

**Chapter Three: Navigating Challenges**    **59**
Facing Obstacles and Criticism    59
Impact and Recognition    71

**Chapter Four: Beyond Business**    **85**
Philanthropy and Social Responsibility    85
Sharing Wisdom and Inspiring Others    97

**Chapter Five: Legacy and Future**    **109**
Building a Lasting Legacy    109
Looking Ahead    122

**Conclusion**    **135**
Sage Yamamoto's Impact on the Tech Industry    135

**Index**    **147**

# Introduction

## The Rise of Mindful Tech

### The Impact of Technology on Society

The impact of technology on society is a multifaceted phenomenon that has transformed every aspect of human life, from communication and education to health care and entertainment. The rapid advancement of technology has led to significant changes in how individuals interact with each other and their environment, creating both opportunities and challenges that warrant careful examination.

### Communication Revolution

One of the most profound impacts of technology is observed in the realm of communication. The advent of the internet and mobile technology has revolutionized the way people connect. According to the *Digital 2023 Global Overview Report*, there are over 5 billion internet users worldwide, facilitating instantaneous communication across vast distances. This connectivity has fostered a global village where information is shared in real-time, enabling social movements and collective action, such as the Arab Spring and the #MeToo movement.

However, this communication revolution is not without its drawbacks. The phenomenon of *echo chambers*, where individuals are exposed only to information that reinforces their existing beliefs, has led to increased polarization in society. A study by Sunstein (2001) highlights how social media algorithms can create feedback loops that isolate users from diverse perspectives, thereby undermining democratic discourse.

## Economic Transformation

Technology has also transformed the economy, leading to the rise of the gig economy and remote work. Platforms like Uber and Upwork have enabled individuals to monetize their skills flexibly. According to a report by the McKinsey Global Institute (2019), up to 162 million people in the United States engage in some form of independent work. This shift has provided opportunities for many, yet it has also raised concerns regarding job security and benefits, as gig workers often lack access to traditional employment protections.

The equation for assessing the economic impact of technology can be represented as:

$$\text{Economic Impact} = \text{Productivity Gains} - \text{Job Displacement}$$

Where productivity gains often arise from automation and efficiency, but these may come at the cost of job displacement in traditional sectors.

## Health and Well-being

In the health sector, technology has enabled significant advancements in medical research, diagnostics, and patient care. Innovations such as telemedicine and wearable health devices have improved access to healthcare services, particularly in underserved areas. The World Health Organization (2020) reported that telehealth services increased by over 150% during the COVID-19 pandemic, highlighting the potential for technology to bridge gaps in healthcare delivery.

Nonetheless, the integration of technology in healthcare also poses ethical dilemmas. The use of artificial intelligence (AI) in medical decision-making raises concerns about bias and accountability. A study by Obermeyer et al. (2019) found that an AI algorithm used in healthcare was less accurate for patients from minority backgrounds, underscoring the importance of ensuring equity in technological advancements.

## Education and Learning

Technology has reshaped education, making learning more accessible and personalized. Online platforms such as Coursera and Khan Academy have democratized access to knowledge, allowing learners from diverse backgrounds to acquire new skills. The *2021 Global Education Monitoring Report* indicates that online learning can enhance educational outcomes, particularly in low-income regions.

However, the digital divide remains a significant challenge. According to the International Telecommunication Union (2021), approximately 2.9 billion people worldwide still lack internet access, hindering their ability to benefit from technological advancements in education. This disparity raises critical questions about equity and inclusion in the digital age.

## Environmental Considerations

The environmental impact of technology is another crucial aspect of its societal influence. While technology has the potential to facilitate sustainable practices—such as smart grids and renewable energy solutions—it also contributes to environmental degradation through electronic waste and resource depletion. The United Nations estimates that the world generates around 53.6 million metric tons of e-waste annually, with only 17.4% being recycled (United Nations, 2020).

The challenge lies in balancing technological advancement with environmental sustainability. The equation for assessing the ecological impact of technology can be expressed as:

$$\text{Ecological Impact} = \text{Resource Consumption} + \text{Waste Generation}$$

This equation highlights the need for mindful innovation that prioritizes sustainability in technological development.

## Conclusion

In conclusion, the impact of technology on society is a double-edged sword, offering both remarkable benefits and significant challenges. As we navigate this complex landscape, it is imperative to foster a culture of ethical innovation that prioritizes the well-being of individuals and communities. By understanding the multifaceted effects of technology, we can work towards a future where technological advancements are aligned with ethical considerations and societal needs.

## The Need for Ethical Innovation

In an era where technology permeates every aspect of our lives, the need for ethical innovation has never been more pressing. As advancements in artificial intelligence, biotechnology, and data analytics accelerate, the implications of these technologies on society raise critical ethical questions. The rapid pace of innovation often outstrips the ability of regulatory frameworks to keep up, leading to a landscape fraught with potential harms.

## Theoretical Foundations

The concept of ethical innovation can be grounded in several philosophical frameworks. Utilitarianism, for instance, posits that the best action is the one that maximizes utility, often defined as that which produces the greatest well-being of the greatest number of people. However, in practice, this can lead to ethical dilemmas where the needs of the few are sacrificed for the many.

Conversely, deontological ethics, as espoused by Immanuel Kant, emphasizes the importance of duty and adherence to moral rules. This perspective insists that certain actions are inherently right or wrong, regardless of their outcomes. For example, the implementation of surveillance technologies raises questions about privacy rights, which some may argue are inviolable, regardless of the potential benefits of increased security.

## Emerging Problems

The absence of ethical considerations in technological innovation can lead to significant societal issues. One prominent example is the use of algorithmic decision-making in hiring practices. Research has shown that algorithms can perpetuate biases present in training data, leading to discriminatory practices that disproportionately affect marginalized groups.

$$\text{Bias}_{\text{algorithm}} = \frac{\text{Number of biased outcomes}}{\text{Total outcomes}} \tag{1}$$

This equation illustrates how the bias in algorithms can be quantitatively assessed, underscoring the need for ethical oversight in their development.

Additionally, the rise of social media platforms has created an environment where misinformation can spread rapidly, influencing public opinion and undermining democratic processes. The ethical implications of content moderation practices and the responsibilities of tech companies in curbing harmful content have become central to discussions about the role of technology in society.

## Examples of Ethical Failures

Several high-profile cases highlight the urgent need for ethical innovation. The Cambridge Analytica scandal serves as a cautionary tale, where personal data from millions of Facebook users was harvested without consent and used to influence electoral outcomes. This incident not only violated privacy rights but also raised questions about the ethical responsibilities of tech companies in safeguarding user data.

Moreover, the deployment of facial recognition technology has sparked widespread debate about surveillance and civil liberties. Instances of wrongful arrests and racial profiling have been linked to flawed algorithms, prompting calls for stricter regulations and ethical guidelines governing the use of such technologies.

## The Role of Ethical Innovation

In response to these challenges, ethical innovation seeks to integrate moral considerations into the technological development process. This involves a proactive approach where ethical implications are assessed at every stage of innovation, from conception to implementation.

Organizations like the IEEE and the Partnership on AI are leading efforts to establish ethical standards and frameworks for technology development. Their initiatives emphasize the importance of transparency, accountability, and inclusivity in creating technologies that serve the public good.

$$\text{Ethical Innovation} = \frac{\text{Transparency} + \text{Accountability} + \text{Inclusivity}}{3} \quad (2)$$

This equation encapsulates the foundational elements of ethical innovation, suggesting that a balanced approach can lead to more responsible technological advancements.

## Conclusion

The need for ethical innovation is not merely an academic exercise but a societal imperative. As we navigate the complexities of a technology-driven world, the integration of ethical considerations into innovation processes is crucial for fostering trust and ensuring that technology serves humanity rather than undermines it. By prioritizing ethical innovation, we can create a future where technology enhances our lives while respecting our rights and values.

## Sage Yamamoto - A Visionary Mind

Sage Yamamoto emerged as a pivotal figure in the realm of ethical technology, embodying the principles of mindfulness and innovation. Born into a family steeped in the tech industry, Sage's early exposure to technology was coupled with a strong emphasis on ethical considerations, setting the stage for a career that would challenge conventional paradigms.

## The Intersection of Technology and Humanity

Yamamoto's vision can be traced back to his formative years, where he recognized the growing chasm between technological advancement and its ethical implications. In an age where technology often outpaces ethical discourse, Sage posited that innovation should not only serve profit but also promote human well-being. This perspective aligns with the ethical theory of *Utilitarianism*, which advocates for actions that maximize overall happiness. Sage's approach can be encapsulated in the equation:

$$H = \sum_{i=1}^{n} U_i \qquad (3)$$

where $H$ represents the total happiness generated by a technological innovation, and $U_i$ denotes the utility derived by each individual affected by the technology. This equation illustrates Yamamoto's commitment to ensuring that technological advancements contribute positively to society at large.

## Challenges in Ethical Innovation

Despite his visionary outlook, Yamamoto faced numerous challenges in promoting ethical technology. One significant hurdle was the pervasive culture within tech industries that prioritized rapid growth and profitability over ethical considerations. For instance, the rise of social media platforms has often been accompanied by issues such as misinformation and mental health concerns. Yamamoto argued that the design of these platforms could be reimagined to prioritize user well-being, advocating for features that encourage positive interactions and reduce harmful content.

This challenge is exemplified by the *Facebook Algorithm Controversy*, where algorithms designed to maximize engagement inadvertently promoted divisive content. Yamamoto's vision sought to rectify such issues by integrating ethical frameworks into algorithm design, emphasizing transparency and accountability.

## Innovative Solutions and Ethical Frameworks

In response to the ethical dilemmas posed by modern technology, Yamamoto developed a set of principles that guided his innovations. These principles include:

- **Transparency:** Users should have clear insights into how their data is used and how algorithms affect their experiences.
- **User Empowerment:** Technologies should empower users to make informed choices, fostering a sense of agency rather than dependency.
- **Sustainability:** Innovations must consider their long-term impact on society and the environment, promoting practices that support ecological balance.

By adhering to these principles, Yamamoto's initiatives aimed to create a tech landscape that prioritizes ethical considerations alongside innovation.

## Impact of Sage Yamamoto's Vision

Yamamoto's influence can be seen in various sectors, from education to healthcare. For instance, his redesign of educational platforms integrated mindfulness practices, encouraging students to engage with content in a way that promotes mental well-being. This approach not only improved academic performance but also fostered a healthier learning environment.

Furthermore, in healthcare, Yamamoto's innovations led to the development of applications that prioritize patient privacy and data security, addressing the growing concerns surrounding digital health records. By employing robust encryption methods and transparent data-sharing policies, these applications exemplified how ethical considerations could be seamlessly integrated into technological advancements.

## Conclusion

In conclusion, Sage Yamamoto stands as a beacon of ethical innovation in the tech industry. His visionary mindset, rooted in a commitment to mindfulness and ethical responsibility, challenges the status quo and inspires a new generation of innovators. As technology continues to evolve, Yamamoto's principles serve as a guiding framework for creating a future where ethical considerations are at the forefront of technological advancement. By fostering a culture of mindfulness in tech, he not only addresses the immediate challenges of the industry but also paves the way for a more equitable and sustainable future.

# Chapter One: A Curious Mind

## Early Life and Influences

### Childhood in a Tech-Oriented Family

Sage Yamamoto was born into a family that epitomized the intersection of technology and innovation. His parents, both engineers, were early adopters of technology, constantly experimenting with the latest gadgets and software. This environment fostered a sense of curiosity and exploration in young Sage, who was surrounded by discussions of algorithms, coding languages, and the latest advancements in artificial intelligence from an early age.

Growing up in a tech-oriented household meant that Sage was exposed to the practical applications of technology beyond mere consumerism. His parents often engaged him in projects that involved building small robots or coding simple games, which laid the foundation for his understanding of how technology could be harnessed to solve real-world problems. This hands-on experience was critical in shaping his analytical skills and igniting his passion for innovation.

$$\text{Curiosity} = \frac{\text{Exposure to Technology} \times \text{Parental Engagement}}{\text{Age}} \qquad (4)$$

This equation illustrates how Sage's curiosity was directly proportional to his exposure to technology and the active engagement of his parents, while inversely related to his age. As he grew older, his cognitive abilities allowed him to grasp more complex concepts, further fueling his interest in the ethical implications of technology.

However, being raised in such an environment also presented challenges. Sage often felt the pressure to excel in a field that was rapidly evolving, where the benchmarks for success were constantly shifting. The competitive nature of the tech industry was palpable, and he witnessed firsthand the ethical dilemmas that arose from technological advancements, such as privacy concerns and the digital divide. These issues were not abstract to him; they were part of family discussions at the dinner table.

For example, when Sage was just ten years old, his parents brought home a new smartphone. While most children were excited about the games and apps, Sage was intrigued by the underlying technology. He began to question how the device collected user data and what that meant for privacy. This early questioning laid the groundwork for his later pursuits in ethical technology, as he recognized the potential for misuse of personal information.

Moreover, the tech-oriented atmosphere of Sage's childhood was not limited to his immediate family. He was part of a community of like-minded families who shared a passion for technology. This community often organized workshops and hackathons, where children were encouraged to collaborate on projects. Sage thrived in this environment, where he learned the value of teamwork and the importance of diverse perspectives in problem-solving.

As Sage navigated his formative years, he also encountered the concept of *digital citizenship*, which encompasses the norms of appropriate and responsible technology use. His parents instilled in him the importance of using technology for positive social impact, emphasizing that with great power comes great responsibility. This principle would later become a cornerstone of his philosophy as an innovator.

In summary, Sage Yamamoto's childhood in a tech-oriented family was a crucible for his future endeavors. The combination of hands-on experiences, ethical discussions, and community engagement fostered a deep understanding of technology's potential and pitfalls. As he matured, these early influences would culminate in a commitment to mindful tech—an approach that balances innovation with ethical responsibility. The foundation laid in his youth would serve as a guiding light throughout his career, shaping his vision for a more ethical and inclusive technological future.

## Discovering a Passion for Science and Ethics

Sage Yamamoto's journey towards a profound understanding of science and ethics began in the fertile ground of his childhood, where curiosity and moral contemplation were nurtured side by side. Growing up in a tech-oriented family, Sage was surrounded by discussions about technological advancements and their implications. This environment laid the groundwork for his dual passion: a fascination with the mechanics of technology and a deep-seated concern for its ethical ramifications.

## The Intersection of Science and Ethics

The interplay between science and ethics is not merely an academic concern; it is a fundamental aspect of how innovations are conceived and implemented. As Sage explored this intersection, he encountered various ethical theories that would shape his outlook. For instance, utilitarianism, which advocates for actions that maximize overall happiness, posed questions about the consequences of technological advancements. Would the benefits of a new technology outweigh the potential harms?

This inquiry led Sage to consider the works of philosophers such as John Stuart Mill, who argued that the greatest happiness principle should guide ethical decision-making. In contrast, deontological ethics, as proposed by Immanuel Kant, emphasized the importance of duty and moral rules, suggesting that certain actions are inherently right or wrong, regardless of their outcomes. This dichotomy sparked Sage's interest in how technological innovations could be aligned with ethical principles.

## Real-World Implications

Sage's academic pursuits were not confined to theoretical discussions; he sought real-world implications of ethical considerations in technology. For example, he became acutely aware of the ethical dilemmas surrounding artificial intelligence (AI). The development of AI systems raised significant questions about accountability, bias, and the potential for misuse. Sage often pondered:

$$\text{Ethical AI} = \text{Transparency} + \text{Fairness} + \text{Accountability} \qquad (5)$$

This equation encapsulated his belief that for AI to be ethical, it must be transparent in its operations, fair in its outcomes, and accountable to its users. The realization that technology could either uplift or harm society depending on its ethical framework fueled Sage's passion for creating mindful tech solutions.

## Influential Experiences

During his formative years, Sage participated in science fairs and technology competitions, where he often incorporated ethical considerations into his projects. One notable project involved designing a prototype for a social media platform that prioritized user mental health. Sage's design philosophy was rooted in the understanding that technology should enhance human well-being rather than detract from it.

For instance, he integrated features that encouraged users to take breaks, provided resources for mental health support, and minimized addictive design elements. This project not only won accolades but also solidified Sage's belief that ethical considerations could drive innovation.

## Mentorship and Guidance

Sage's mentors played a pivotal role in shaping his understanding of science and ethics. One of his most influential mentors was Dr. Elena Torres, a leading ethicist in technology. Dr. Torres introduced Sage to the concept of "ethical design," which emphasizes the responsibility of technologists to consider the broader societal implications of their work. Under her guidance, Sage learned to ask critical questions about the technologies he encountered:

- Who benefits from this technology?
- What are the potential harms?
- How can we mitigate negative impacts?

These questions became a guiding framework for Sage as he navigated his academic and professional journey.

## A Commitment to Ethical Innovation

By the time Sage reached college, his passion for science and ethics had crystallized into a commitment to ethical innovation. He recognized that as technology continued to evolve at a rapid pace, the need for ethical frameworks would become increasingly urgent. This realization motivated him to pursue a degree in computer science, where he could blend technical expertise with ethical considerations.

In his college years, Sage actively sought out courses and projects that aligned with his values. He became involved in initiatives aimed at promoting digital literacy and ethical tech practices among his peers. Through workshops and discussions, he advocated for a culture of mindfulness in technology, emphasizing that ethical innovation is not a hindrance to progress but a necessary component of it.

In summary, Sage Yamamoto's discovery of his passion for science and ethics was a multifaceted journey influenced by his upbringing, academic pursuits, and mentorship. This foundation would ultimately empower him to disrupt the tech industry with a vision of mindful technology that prioritizes ethical considerations alongside innovation. As he moved forward, the lessons learned during this critical period would continue to inform his work and inspire others in the field of ethical tech.

## Meeting Mentors and Role Models

Sage Yamamoto's journey into the realm of mindful technology was significantly shaped by the mentors and role models he encountered along the way. These influential figures not only provided guidance but also instilled in him the values of ethical innovation and social responsibility. This section explores the pivotal relationships that helped mold Sage's vision and approach to technology.

## The Importance of Mentorship

Mentorship plays a crucial role in personal and professional development, particularly in fields as dynamic and impactful as technology. According to Kram's (1985) theory of mentoring, the relationship between a mentor and a mentee can be categorized into two main functions: career development and psychosocial support. Career development encompasses sponsorship, exposure, and coaching, while psychosocial support includes friendship, acceptance, and emotional support.

For Sage, mentors served as both career guides and emotional anchors, helping him navigate the complexities of the tech industry while remaining grounded in his ethical principles.

## Early Influences

During his formative years, Sage was fortunate to meet several key figures who inspired him to explore the intersection of technology and ethics. One of his early mentors was Dr. Evelyn Chen, a renowned computer scientist and advocate for ethical AI. Dr. Chen introduced Sage to the concept of *algorithmic bias*, emphasizing how technology can inadvertently perpetuate inequalities. She often quoted the famous phrase, "With great power comes great responsibility," which resonated deeply with Sage.

This lesson became foundational in Sage's understanding of the ethical implications of technology. He learned that every line of code has the potential to impact lives, and thus, it is imperative to approach innovation with a mindful perspective.

## Role Models in the Field

In addition to Dr. Chen, Sage sought inspiration from various role models who embodied the principles of ethical innovation. One such figure was Tim Berners-Lee, the inventor of the World Wide Web. Sage admired Berners-Lee's commitment to an open and accessible internet, which he viewed as a powerful tool for democratizing information. Berners-Lee's advocacy for web standards and privacy rights became a guiding light for Sage as he sought to develop technologies that prioritize user agency and ethical considerations.

Another influential role model was Sheryl Sandberg, whose work in technology and advocacy for women in leadership positions resonated with Sage. Sandberg's book, *Lean In*, inspired him to recognize the importance of diversity in tech, not only for ethical reasons but also for fostering innovation. Sage internalized the idea that diverse teams lead to better problem-solving and more inclusive products.

## Networking and Community Engagement

As Sage progressed through his education, he actively sought opportunities to engage with mentors and role models in various capacities. He attended technology conferences, workshops, and seminars where he could interact with industry leaders. One notable event was the *Ethical Tech Summit*, where he had the chance to meet pioneers in the field of responsible technology.

At the summit, Sage participated in a panel discussion on the ethical implications of emerging technologies. He was particularly influenced by a conversation with Dr. Kate Crawford, a leading researcher on the social implications of AI. Dr. Crawford's insights on the need for transparency and accountability in AI systems reinforced Sage's commitment to ethical innovation.

## The Ripple Effect of Mentorship

The influence of mentors extended beyond personal growth; it also shaped Sage's vision for his future endeavors. Inspired by the guidance he received, Sage became determined to create a supportive environment for aspiring innovators. He established a mentorship program within his startup, Mindful Tech Solutions, aimed at fostering the next generation of ethical technologists.

This program not only provided mentorship but also emphasized the importance of ethical considerations in technology development. Participants engaged in workshops that addressed real-world challenges, encouraging them to think critically about the societal impacts of their work.

## Conclusion

The relationships Sage Yamamoto built with mentors and role models were instrumental in shaping his approach to mindful technology. Through their guidance, he learned the significance of ethical innovation and the responsibility that comes with technological advancement. As he moved forward in his career, Sage carried these lessons with him, committed to fostering a culture of ethical responsibility in the tech industry. Ultimately, the impact of these mentors extended beyond Sage; it rippled through the community he sought to inspire, creating a legacy of mindful innovation.

## Exploring the Intersection of Technology and Humanity

The intersection of technology and humanity represents a critical juncture in the evolution of society. As we advance into an era dominated by digital innovation, understanding this relationship becomes paramount. This section delves into the philosophical and practical implications of technology in our daily lives, particularly focusing on how ethical considerations must guide technological advancements.

## Philosophical Foundations

To grasp the intersection of technology and humanity, we must first explore the philosophical underpinnings that frame our understanding of both entities. The works of Martin Heidegger, particularly his essay "The Question Concerning Technology," provide a foundational perspective. Heidegger argues that technology is not merely a collection of tools; it shapes our understanding of the world and ourselves. He introduces the concept of *Gestell*, or "enframing," which suggests that technology organizes our perception of reality, often reducing the complexity of human experience to mere data points.

In contrast, Sherry Turkle, in her book "Alone Together," argues that technology can create a facade of connectivity while simultaneously fostering isolation. Turkle's insights highlight the paradox of our digital age: while we are more connected than ever, our relationships may become superficial, leading to a disconnection from our authentic selves. This duality presents a challenge that innovators like Sage Yamamoto aim to address through mindful technology.

## Ethical Considerations

The ethical implications of technology are vast and complex. As Sage Yamamoto recognized, the rapid pace of technological advancement often outstrips our ability to understand its impact on humanity. This dissonance can lead to several critical issues:

- **Privacy Concerns:** The collection and analysis of personal data raise significant ethical questions. As technology companies collect vast amounts of user data, the potential for misuse increases. The Cambridge Analytica scandal serves as a poignant example, where data harvested from social media was used to influence political outcomes without users' consent.

- **Algorithmic Bias:** Algorithms that drive decision-making processes can perpetuate existing biases if not carefully monitored. For instance, facial recognition technology has been shown to misidentify individuals from minority groups at higher rates than their counterparts. This raises questions about the fairness and accountability of technology in critical areas such as law enforcement and hiring practices.

- **Mental Health Implications:** The design of social media platforms often prioritizes engagement over user well-being. Research indicates that excessive use of social media can lead to anxiety, depression, and a distorted sense of reality. Innovators must consider how technology can be designed to promote mental health rather than detract from it.

## Examples of Ethical Innovations

Sage Yamamoto's approach to mindful technology illustrates how ethical considerations can be integrated into technological development. A few notable examples include:

1. **Mindful Social Media Platforms:** Yamamoto's team developed a social media platform that incorporates features designed to promote positive interactions and mental well-being. By implementing algorithms that prioritize meaningful connections over sensational content, the platform seeks to enhance user experience while minimizing harmful effects.

2. **Ethical AI Development:** Recognizing the potential for bias in AI systems, Yamamoto's startup established a framework for ethical AI development. This framework includes diverse training data and regular audits to ensure fairness and accountability in AI applications, particularly in sensitive areas such as hiring and law enforcement.

3. **Health Tech Solutions:** In the healthcare sector, Yamamoto's innovations focus on patient-centered technologies that respect privacy and enhance patient autonomy. For example, telehealth solutions that prioritize secure data sharing empower patients to take control of their health information while ensuring confidentiality.

## The Future of Technology and Humanity

As we look to the future, the relationship between technology and humanity will continue to evolve. The challenge lies in ensuring that technological advancements serve to enhance the human experience rather than diminish it. This requires a concerted effort from innovators, ethicists, and policymakers to create frameworks that prioritize ethical considerations in technology development.

The concept of *Human-Centered Design* emerges as a guiding principle in this endeavor. By placing human needs and values at the forefront of technological innovation, we can create tools that enrich our lives while addressing the ethical dilemmas posed by rapid advancements. This approach emphasizes empathy, inclusivity, and sustainability, ensuring that technology serves as a bridge rather than a barrier between individuals and their communities.

In conclusion, exploring the intersection of technology and humanity reveals a complex landscape filled with both challenges and opportunities. As Sage Yamamoto exemplifies, mindful innovation can lead to ethical advancements that enhance our society. The ongoing dialogue between technology and humanity will be crucial in shaping a future where technology empowers rather than alienates, fostering a more equitable and compassionate world.

## Recognizing the Ethical Implications of Technological Advancements

As Sage Yamamoto navigated the complex landscape of technology during her formative years, she became acutely aware of the ethical implications that accompany rapid technological advancements. The integration of technology into daily life has transformed society in unprecedented ways, but it has also raised significant ethical concerns that demand careful consideration. This section explores the multifaceted ethical dilemmas that arise from technological progress and emphasizes the importance of addressing these issues proactively.

## The Dual-Edged Sword of Innovation

Technological advancements often present a dual-edged sword. On one hand, innovations can lead to significant improvements in quality of life, efficiency, and connectivity. On the other hand, they can exacerbate existing inequalities, infringe on privacy rights, and create new forms of harm. For instance, while social media platforms have revolutionized communication, they have also been linked to mental health issues, cyberbullying, and the spread of misinformation. The challenge lies in balancing these benefits with the potential for adverse consequences.

## Ethical Theories in Technology

To navigate the ethical landscape of technology, it is essential to apply various ethical theories.

- **Utilitarianism:** This theory suggests that the best action is the one that maximizes overall happiness. In technology, utilitarianism can guide decisions about product development by evaluating the potential benefits and harms to the greatest number of people. For example, when developing an AI system for healthcare, the goal would be to enhance patient outcomes while minimizing risks associated with data privacy.

- **Deontological Ethics:** Deontological theories focus on the morality of actions themselves rather than their consequences. This perspective emphasizes the importance of adhering to ethical principles, such as honesty and respect for individuals' rights. For instance, a tech company might prioritize user consent and transparency in data collection practices, regardless of potential profit maximization.

- **Virtue Ethics:** This approach emphasizes the character and virtues of the decision-makers. In the context of technology, fostering a culture of integrity, responsibility, and empathy among developers and leaders can lead to more ethical innovations. Companies like Mindful Tech Solutions, founded by Yamamoto, exemplify this approach by embedding ethical considerations into their corporate values.

## Real-World Ethical Dilemmas

Several real-world scenarios illustrate the ethical implications of technological advancements:

- **Data Privacy:** The Cambridge Analytica scandal is a prime example of how data misuse can undermine public trust. The unauthorized harvesting of personal data from millions of users raised questions about consent and privacy, highlighting the need for ethical data management practices.

- **AI and Bias:** Algorithms used in AI systems can perpetuate existing biases if not carefully designed. For instance, facial recognition technology has been shown to exhibit racial and gender biases, leading to wrongful accusations and discrimination. Recognizing these biases is crucial for developing fair and equitable technology.

- **Automation and Employment:** The rise of automation poses ethical questions regarding job displacement. While automation can increase efficiency, it can also lead to significant job losses in certain sectors. The ethical implications of prioritizing profit over people must be addressed by considering retraining programs and social safety nets.

## The Role of Ethical Frameworks

To address these ethical implications, organizations must adopt comprehensive ethical frameworks that guide decision-making processes. Such frameworks should include:

- **Stakeholder Engagement:** Involving diverse stakeholders in the development process ensures that multiple perspectives are considered. This can help identify potential ethical concerns early on and foster a sense of shared responsibility.

- **Transparency and Accountability:** Companies should prioritize transparency in their operations, particularly regarding data practices and algorithmic decisions. Establishing accountability mechanisms can help build trust and ensure ethical compliance.

- **Continuous Ethical Education:** As technology evolves, so too must the understanding of its ethical implications. Ongoing education and training for employees can create a culture of ethical awareness and responsiveness.

## Conclusion

Recognizing the ethical implications of technological advancements is not merely a theoretical exercise; it is a practical necessity for innovators like Sage Yamamoto. By understanding the ethical landscape and integrating ethical considerations into the design and implementation of technology, innovators can create solutions that not only advance society but do so in a manner that is just, equitable, and respectful of human dignity. As technology continues to evolve, the call for ethical mindfulness in innovation will only grow louder, demanding a proactive approach to ensure that progress serves the greater good.

# The College Years

## Pursuing a Degree in Computer Science

Sage Yamamoto embarked on his academic journey by enrolling in a prestigious university to pursue a degree in Computer Science. This decision was not merely a pursuit of technical knowledge but a conscious choice to delve into the ethical implications of technology. The curriculum offered a rich blend of theoretical foundations and practical applications, which would later serve as the bedrock for his innovative endeavors in mindful tech.

## Foundational Knowledge

In the first year, Sage was introduced to the core principles of computer science, including algorithms, data structures, and programming languages. He learned that algorithms are not just sequences of instructions but can be viewed through the lens of efficiency and ethics. For example, the time complexity of an algorithm is often expressed using Big O notation:

$$O(n) \quad \text{(linear time complexity)} \qquad (6)$$

Understanding the efficiency of algorithms was crucial, as Sage realized that the choices made in algorithm design could have far-reaching implications on resource consumption and environmental sustainability. This realization prompted him to consider how mindful tech could optimize algorithms to reduce energy usage in data centers, which are notorious for their high carbon footprints.

## Ethical Considerations in Technology

As Sage progressed through his studies, he encountered courses that challenged him to think critically about the ethical considerations of technology. One pivotal course focused on the societal impacts of artificial intelligence (AI) and machine

# THE COLLEGE YEARS 21

learning. Sage learned about the biases that can be encoded in algorithms, leading to discriminatory outcomes in areas such as hiring practices and criminal justice.

For instance, he studied the case of a hiring algorithm that favored candidates from certain demographics, leading to a lack of diversity in the workplace. This sparked a debate among his peers about the responsibility of technologists to ensure fairness and equity in their designs. Sage became passionate about integrating ethical frameworks into the development of AI systems, advocating for transparency and accountability.

## Collaboration and Innovation

During his college years, Sage actively sought collaboration with fellow students who shared his vision of ethical innovation. He was instrumental in forming a student organization focused on ethical tech, where members would discuss the latest advancements and their implications. This collaborative environment fostered creativity and innovation, allowing Sage to explore projects that combined technology with social good.

One notable project involved developing a mobile application designed to promote mental well-being among students. The app utilized mindfulness techniques and provided users with tools to manage stress and anxiety. Sage and his team conducted user research to ensure the app was inclusive and accessible, demonstrating their commitment to ethical design practices.

## Networking with Ethical Thinkers

Sage also made it a priority to connect with mentors and industry professionals who were leaders in the field of ethical technology. He attended conferences and workshops where he engaged with thought leaders discussing the importance of ethics in tech. These interactions not only expanded his knowledge but also reinforced his belief in the necessity of ethical innovation.

One memorable encounter was with a prominent figure in the tech industry who spoke about the importance of incorporating ethical considerations into product development. This experience solidified Sage's resolve to pursue a career that prioritized ethical practices, inspiring him to envision a future where technology serves humanity responsibly.

## Conclusion

In conclusion, Sage Yamamoto's pursuit of a degree in Computer Science was marked by a commitment to ethical innovation. Through foundational knowledge, critical engagement with ethical dilemmas, collaboration with like-minded peers, and networking with industry leaders, Sage laid the groundwork for his future endeavors in mindful tech. His academic journey was not just about acquiring technical skills but about shaping a vision for a more responsible and ethical technological landscape.

## Exploring Ethical Considerations in Technology

As Sage Yamamoto embarked on her academic journey in computer science, she quickly recognized that technology is not just a collection of algorithms and hardware, but a powerful tool that can shape human experience and societal structures. This realization prompted her to delve into the ethical considerations inherent in technological development. The exploration of ethics in technology encompasses a wide range of issues, including privacy, consent, bias, and the broader implications of automation and artificial intelligence (AI).

## Theoretical Frameworks

To navigate the complex landscape of ethical considerations, Sage drew upon several philosophical theories. One of the primary frameworks she studied was *Utilitarianism*, which posits that the best action is the one that maximizes overall happiness or utility. This approach is particularly relevant in technology, where decisions often impact large populations. However, Sage also recognized the limitations of utilitarianism, especially in cases where the majority's happiness could infringe on the rights of minorities.

In contrast, the *Deontological* perspective, primarily associated with Immanuel Kant, emphasizes the importance of duty and adherence to moral rules. This approach advocates for the protection of individual rights regardless of the outcomes, which resonated with Sage's vision of ethical technology. For instance, when designing algorithms for social media platforms, she was mindful of the potential for these technologies to manipulate user behavior, raising questions about consent and autonomy.

## Key Ethical Issues

**Privacy**   One of the most pressing ethical concerns in technology is privacy. The rise of data-driven technologies has led to unprecedented levels of data collection, often without explicit user consent. Sage became acutely aware of the implications of this practice during her studies. She examined the Cambridge Analytica scandal, where data harvested from millions of Facebook users was used to influence political campaigns. This incident highlighted the need for robust privacy protections and ethical standards in data handling.

**Bias and Fairness**   Another critical area of concern is algorithmic bias. As Sage explored machine learning models, she learned that these systems can inadvertently perpetuate existing societal biases. For example, facial recognition technology has been shown to misidentify individuals from minority groups at higher rates than their white counterparts. This raises ethical questions about fairness and equality in technology deployment. Sage advocated for diverse data sets and inclusive design practices to mitigate bias in technological solutions.

**Automation and Employment**   The rise of automation and AI presents another ethical dilemma: the impact on employment. While these technologies can enhance efficiency and productivity, they also threaten job displacement for millions of workers. Sage engaged in discussions about the moral responsibility of technologists to consider the societal implications of their innovations. She explored potential solutions, such as reskilling programs and universal basic income (UBI), to address the challenges posed by automation.

## Case Studies

Sage's academic work included several case studies that exemplified these ethical considerations. One notable example was her analysis of the deployment of AI in hiring processes. Many companies began using AI to screen resumes, but Sage discovered that these systems often favored candidates based on historical hiring data, which may reflect biases against certain demographics. She proposed a framework for ethical hiring practices that included transparency in AI decision-making and regular audits to ensure fairness.

Another case study involved the ethical implications of social media algorithms. Sage examined how platforms like Instagram and TikTok prioritize content based on engagement metrics, often leading to harmful effects on users' mental health. She argued for the redesign of these algorithms to promote content that fosters well-being rather than simply maximizing engagement.

## Conclusion

Through her exploration of ethical considerations in technology, Sage Yamamoto laid the groundwork for her future innovations in mindful tech. She recognized that ethical dilemmas are not merely obstacles but opportunities for creating more responsible and inclusive technological solutions. By integrating ethical frameworks into her work, Sage aimed to ensure that technology serves humanity, rather than undermines it.

As she moved forward in her career, these foundational insights would guide her decisions and inspire her to advocate for a tech industry that prioritizes ethical considerations alongside innovation. The journey through ethical exploration was not just an academic exercise; it was a critical component of her identity as a future innovator in the tech landscape.

## Forming the Foundation for Mindful Tech

During Sage Yamamoto's college years, a pivotal transformation took place as he began to form the foundation for what would eventually become Mindful Tech. This period was characterized by an exploration of the ethical implications of technology, a deepening understanding of the human experience, and a commitment to fostering innovation that prioritized well-being over mere profit.

### Understanding Ethical Frameworks

To establish a robust foundation for Mindful Tech, Sage immersed himself in various ethical frameworks that informed his approach to technology. He studied the works of prominent philosophers such as Immanuel Kant, who emphasized the importance of duty and moral law, and utilitarian thinkers like John Stuart Mill, who advocated for actions that maximize happiness. This intellectual exploration culminated in a personal philosophy that sought to balance technological advancement with ethical responsibility.

$$\text{Utilitarian Principle: Maximize} \sum_{i=1}^{n} U_i \qquad (7)$$

Where $U_i$ represents the utility or happiness derived by individuals from a particular technological innovation. Sage recognized that the goal of technology should not solely be to increase efficiency or profitability but to enhance the quality of life for all stakeholders involved.

### Identifying Key Problems

As Sage delved deeper into the world of technology, he became acutely aware of the pressing problems that needed addressing. The rise of social media, for instance, had led to increased mental health issues among users, particularly among younger demographics. Studies indicated a correlation between excessive social media use and anxiety, depression, and loneliness [?]. This realization fueled Sage's passion for creating solutions that prioritized mental well-being.

## Engaging with Peers and Mentors

Sage's journey was not a solitary one. He actively sought out peers and mentors who shared his vision for ethical innovation. Collaborating with like-minded individuals allowed him to exchange ideas and refine his approach to technology. One of his mentors, Dr. Emily Chen, a leading researcher in technology ethics, introduced him to the concept of *design thinking*, a user-centered approach that emphasizes empathy in the design process. This methodology would later become a cornerstone of Mindful Tech's innovation strategy.

## The Role of Interdisciplinary Collaboration

Recognizing that technology does not exist in a vacuum, Sage championed interdisciplinary collaboration. He brought together students from diverse fields—psychology, sociology, computer science, and design—to form a think tank dedicated to exploring the intersection of technology and humanity. This collaborative environment fostered creativity and innovation, leading to the development of prototypes that addressed real-world issues.

For example, a team project resulted in the creation of an app that encouraged users to take mindful breaks from their screens. The app utilized behavioral prompts and gamification techniques to incentivize users to step away from their devices, ultimately promoting mental well-being.

## Establishing Core Values

As the groundwork for Mindful Tech solidified, Sage and his team articulated a set of core values that would guide their innovations. These values included:

- **Empathy:** Understanding the needs and experiences of users.

- **Transparency:** Being open about data usage and business practices.

- **Sustainability:** Prioritizing environmental considerations in all technological solutions.

- **Inclusivity:** Ensuring that innovations benefit diverse populations.

These core values not only shaped the company's culture but also served as a compass for decision-making as they navigated the complex landscape of the tech industry.

### Creating a Prototype for Mindful Tech

With a clear vision and a dedicated team, Sage initiated the development of a prototype that embodied the principles of Mindful Tech. This prototype, a platform designed to facilitate mindful interactions among users, integrated features such as guided meditations, community support groups, and tools for tracking emotional well-being. The design process emphasized user feedback, ensuring that the final product resonated with the target audience.

### Testing and Iteration

The testing phase was crucial for refining the platform. Sage and his team conducted user interviews and usability tests to gather insights on the prototype's effectiveness. Feedback revealed areas for improvement, such as enhancing the user interface for greater accessibility and adding features that fostered community engagement.

Through iterative design, the team was able to create a more intuitive and impactful product. This commitment to continuous improvement became a hallmark of Mindful Tech's approach, ensuring that their innovations remained relevant and effective.

### Conclusion

Forming the foundation for Mindful Tech was a multifaceted journey that involved understanding ethical frameworks, identifying key problems, engaging with peers and mentors, establishing core values, and creating a prototype that prioritized user well-being. Sage Yamamoto's experiences during his college years laid the groundwork for a company that would disrupt the tech industry by placing ethics and mindfulness at the forefront of innovation. As Mindful Tech began to take shape, it became clear that the future of technology could be both innovative and compassionate, paving the way for a more ethical digital landscape.

## Fostering a Culture of Collaboration and Innovation

In the rapidly evolving landscape of technology, fostering a culture of collaboration and innovation is paramount for success. Sage Yamamoto recognized early on that the synergy created by diverse teams could lead to groundbreaking solutions that address ethical dilemmas in technology. This section explores the strategies employed by Yamamoto during her college years to cultivate a collaborative environment that nurtured innovation.

## Theoretical Framework

The concept of collaborative innovation is grounded in several theories, including the *Open Innovation* model proposed by Henry Chesbrough, which suggests that organizations can benefit from external ideas and pathways to market. This model emphasizes the importance of integrating knowledge from various sources, enhancing creativity and problem-solving capabilities. The *Social Constructivist Theory* also supports this notion, positing that knowledge is constructed through social interactions, making collaboration essential in educational and professional settings.

## Strategies for Collaboration

Yamamoto implemented several key strategies to foster a culture of collaboration:

- **Interdisciplinary Teams:** By forming teams that included members from various disciplines—such as computer science, ethics, psychology, and design—Yamamoto ensured a rich exchange of ideas. This diversity allowed for a more holistic approach to problem-solving, as team members brought different perspectives and expertise to the table.

- **Open Communication Channels:** Establishing open lines of communication was crucial. Yamamoto encouraged the use of collaborative tools such as Slack and Trello, which facilitated real-time discussions and project management. This transparency helped to break down silos and foster a sense of community among team members.

- **Regular Brainstorming Sessions:** Yamamoto organized weekly brainstorming sessions where team members could freely share ideas without fear of criticism. This practice not only stimulated creativity but also built trust among team members, as they felt valued and heard.

- **Mentorship Programs:** Recognizing the importance of mentorship, Yamamoto paired experienced innovators with newcomers. This not only facilitated knowledge transfer but also created a supportive environment where less experienced members could learn and grow.

- **Celebrating Failures:** Yamamoto understood that failure is an inherent part of innovation. She encouraged her team to view failures as learning opportunities rather than setbacks. This mindset shift fostered resilience and a willingness to take risks, essential ingredients for innovation.

## Challenges Faced

While fostering collaboration and innovation, Yamamoto encountered several challenges:

- **Resistance to Change:** Some team members were accustomed to traditional working methods and were initially resistant to the collaborative approach. To address this, Yamamoto implemented training sessions on the benefits of collaboration and innovation, gradually shifting mindsets.

- **Conflicts in Team Dynamics:** Diverse teams often face conflicts due to differing opinions and work styles. Yamamoto facilitated conflict resolution workshops, teaching team members effective communication strategies to navigate disagreements constructively.

- **Balancing Individual and Team Goals:** Ensuring that individual goals aligned with team objectives proved challenging. Yamamoto introduced regular check-ins to align goals and foster accountability, ensuring that personal aspirations contributed to the collective mission.

## Examples of Successful Collaboration

The collaborative culture fostered by Yamamoto led to several successful innovations:

- **Mindful Social Media Platform:** A team of developers, psychologists, and designers collaborated to create a social media platform that promotes mental well-being. By integrating features that encourage positive interactions and mindfulness, they addressed the ethical implications of social media usage.

- **Ethical AI Framework:** A diverse group of computer scientists and ethicists worked together to develop an ethical framework for AI algorithms. This collaboration resulted in guidelines that prioritize fairness, transparency, and accountability in AI development.

- **Sustainable Tech Initiatives:** Yamamoto's team partnered with environmental scientists to create sustainable technology solutions. Their collaborative efforts led to innovations that reduced e-waste and promoted eco-friendly practices within the tech industry.

## Conclusion

In conclusion, Sage Yamamoto's commitment to fostering a culture of collaboration and innovation during her college years laid the foundation for her future successes in the tech industry. By implementing strategies that emphasized diversity, open communication, and continuous learning, she not only overcame challenges but also created an environment where groundbreaking ideas could flourish. The lessons learned from her experiences serve as a blueprint for aspiring innovators, highlighting the critical role that collaboration plays in ethical technological advancement.

$$\text{Innovation} = f(\text{Collaboration}, \text{Diversity}, \text{Trust}) \qquad (8)$$

This equation encapsulates the essence of Yamamoto's approach, illustrating that innovation is a function of collaborative efforts, diverse perspectives, and a foundation of trust among team members. As we move forward in an increasingly complex technological landscape, embracing these principles will be vital for future innovators seeking to create meaningful change.

## Creating a Network of Ethical Thinkers

In the rapidly evolving landscape of technology, the importance of fostering a community of ethical thinkers cannot be overstated. Sage Yamamoto recognized early on that technology, while a powerful tool for innovation, also carries the potential for significant ethical dilemmas. As he embarked on his academic journey, he understood that collaboration with like-minded individuals would be essential in addressing these challenges.

### Theoretical Framework

The theoretical underpinnings of creating a network of ethical thinkers can be traced back to the concept of *social capital*, which refers to the networks of relationships among people who work in a particular field, enabling that society to function effectively. In the context of technology, social capital facilitates the sharing of knowledge, resources, and ethical considerations that are crucial for responsible innovation. According to Putnam (2000), social capital is a vital component in promoting collective action and fostering trust among individuals, which is especially relevant in the tech industry where collaboration is key to success.

### Identifying Common Values

To build a robust network, it is essential to identify and articulate common values among its members. Sage initiated discussions around core ethical principles such as transparency, accountability, and inclusivity. By establishing a shared understanding of these values, members of the network could align their objectives and work collaboratively towards common goals. This alignment is crucial when addressing ethical dilemmas, as it provides a framework for decision-making that prioritizes the well-being of society over mere profit.

### Challenges in Networking

Despite the benefits of creating a network of ethical thinkers, several challenges persist. One significant issue is the *diversity of thought*. While diversity can enhance creativity and innovation, it can also lead to conflicts when differing ethical perspectives clash. For instance, a startup focused on data privacy may find itself at odds with another organization that prioritizes user engagement through data collection. Sage addressed these challenges by promoting open dialogue and encouraging members to approach disagreements with a mindset of understanding and compromise.

### Practical Examples

To facilitate the creation of this network, Sage organized a series of workshops and seminars that brought together students, industry professionals, and academics. These events served as platforms for sharing ideas, discussing ethical dilemmas, and brainstorming innovative solutions. For example, during one workshop, participants explored the ethical implications of artificial intelligence in healthcare. By engaging in case studies and role-playing scenarios, attendees were able to consider various perspectives and develop strategies for ethical decision-making.

Furthermore, Sage leveraged technology to create an online platform where members could share resources, discuss current ethical issues, and collaborate on projects. This digital space became a vital hub for the community, allowing for continuous engagement and knowledge exchange. One notable project that emerged from this platform was the development of an ethical framework for the use of AI in educational settings, emphasizing the importance of fairness and accessibility.

## The Role of Mentorship

Mentorship played a pivotal role in nurturing the next generation of ethical thinkers within the network. Sage actively sought out experienced professionals to mentor young innovators, providing guidance on navigating ethical challenges in their work. This mentorship not only helped individuals develop their ethical reasoning skills but also fostered a sense of belonging within the community. As a result, many mentees went on to become leaders in their respective fields, further expanding the network and its influence.

## Conclusion

Creating a network of ethical thinkers is a dynamic and ongoing process that requires intentional effort and commitment. Sage Yamamoto's approach to networking emphasized the importance of shared values, open dialogue, and mentorship, which collectively contribute to a culture of ethical innovation. As the technology landscape continues to evolve, the need for such networks will only grow, underscoring the critical role that ethical thinkers play in shaping a responsible and mindful tech future. By investing in these relationships, innovators can ensure that technology serves humanity in a way that is equitable, sustainable, and ethical.

# Chapter Two: Disrupting the Industry

## Creating an Ethical Tech Startup

### The Birth of Mindful Tech Solutions

The inception of Mindful Tech Solutions marked a pivotal moment in the intersection of technology and ethics. Founded by Sage Yamamoto, this startup emerged from a vision to create technology that not only serves users but also respects their well-being and societal values. The initial idea was simple yet profound: to develop technological tools that prioritize mental health, ethical engagement, and user empowerment.

### Identifying the Need

As Sage Yamamoto observed the tech landscape in the early 2020s, a growing concern emerged regarding the negative impacts of technology on mental health. Research indicated a correlation between excessive social media use and issues such as anxiety, depression, and loneliness. According to a study published in the *Journal of Social and Clinical Psychology*, individuals who limited their social media use to 30 minutes a day experienced significant improvements in their well-being. This evidence highlighted the urgent need for a shift in how technology was designed and utilized.

### Formulating the Vision

Sage's vision for Mindful Tech Solutions was rooted in the principles of ethical innovation. Drawing inspiration from philosophers such as Immanuel Kant, who emphasized the importance of treating individuals as ends in themselves rather than means to an end, Sage sought to create a company that would embody these values. The mission statement was clear: "To harness technology for the betterment of humanity by prioritizing ethical considerations in every innovation."

## The Development Process

The development of Mindful Tech Solutions began with a series of brainstorming sessions, where Sage and a group of like-minded innovators gathered to ideate potential products. They employed design thinking methodologies, which emphasize empathy and user-centric design, to ensure that their solutions were tailored to meet the needs of users without compromising their mental health.

$$\text{Design Thinking Process} = \text{Empathize} + \text{Define} + \text{Ideate} + \text{Prototype} + \text{Test}$$

This iterative process allowed the team to refine their ideas continuously. They conducted surveys and focus groups to gather feedback, ensuring that the products developed would genuinely resonate with users.

## Initial Product Offerings

The first product launched by Mindful Tech Solutions was a reimagined social media platform called *MindConnect*. Unlike traditional platforms that often promote addictive behaviors, MindConnect was designed to foster genuine connections and mental well-being. Key features included:

- **Mindful Moments:** A feature that encouraged users to take breaks and engage in mindfulness practices.

- **Connection Metrics:** Instead of tracking likes and shares, users could see metrics related to meaningful interactions and emotional well-being.

- **Community Support:** A dedicated space for users to share experiences and support one another, moderated by mental health professionals.

The launch of MindConnect was met with enthusiasm, and early user feedback indicated a positive shift in user engagement and satisfaction. Users reported feeling more connected and less anxious compared to their experiences on traditional platforms.

## Challenges Faced

Despite the initial success, Mindful Tech Solutions faced several challenges. The tech industry is notoriously competitive, and many established companies viewed Sage's ethical approach as a threat to their profit-driven models. One significant challenge was securing funding from investors who were often focused on short-term gains rather than long-term societal impact.

To address this, Sage and the team crafted a compelling narrative that highlighted the growing consumer demand for ethical technology. They presented data showing that 70% of consumers were willing to pay a premium for products that align with their values, emphasizing the potential for sustainable profitability.

## Building a Brand Identity

To further differentiate themselves in the market, Mindful Tech Solutions focused on building a strong brand identity centered around transparency and community engagement. They implemented policies that encouraged open dialogue with users about product development and ethical practices. Social media campaigns highlighting user testimonials and the positive impact of their products helped to build trust and loyalty among their audience.

## Conclusion

The birth of Mindful Tech Solutions represented a significant step towards reshaping the tech landscape. By prioritizing ethical considerations and user well-being, Sage Yamamoto and her team laid the groundwork for a new paradigm in technology—one that values mindfulness and responsibility alongside innovation. As the company continued to grow, it became clear that the demand for mindful tech was not just a trend but a necessary evolution in the way society engages with technology.

## Assembling a Diverse and Innovative Team

In the rapidly evolving landscape of technology, the importance of assembling a diverse and innovative team cannot be overstated. Sage Yamamoto recognized early on that the key to fostering creativity and ethical innovation lay in the diversity of thought, experience, and background within his startup, Mindful Tech Solutions. This section explores the theoretical underpinnings of team diversity, the challenges faced in assembling such a team, and the tangible benefits that arose from this approach.

## Theoretical Framework

Diversity in teams can be understood through several theoretical lenses, including social identity theory and the theory of cognitive diversity. Social identity theory posits that individuals categorize themselves and others into various social groups, which can influence their behavior and interactions. When teams comprise members from different backgrounds—be it cultural, gender, or socio-economic—there is a broader range of perspectives and experiences, leading to enhanced problem-solving capabilities.

Cognitive diversity theory, on the other hand, emphasizes the value of differing thought processes, problem-solving approaches, and perspectives. Research indicates that teams with cognitive diversity outperform homogenous teams, particularly in complex tasks that require innovative solutions. A study by Page (2007) demonstrated that diverse groups are more likely to arrive at novel solutions than their more uniform counterparts, as they draw from a wider array of knowledge and experiences.

## Challenges in Assembling a Diverse Team

While the benefits of diversity are clear, assembling such a team presents several challenges. One significant barrier is unconscious bias, which can affect hiring decisions and team dynamics. For instance, hiring managers may unconsciously favor candidates who share similar backgrounds or experiences, leading to a lack of diversity in the team. To combat this, Sage implemented structured interviews and blind recruitment processes to minimize biases.

Another challenge lies in the integration of diverse team members. Differences in communication styles, cultural norms, and work ethics can lead to misunderstandings and conflict. For example, a team member from a collectivist culture may prioritize group harmony, while an individual from an individualistic culture may emphasize personal achievement. To address these differences, Sage organized team-building workshops focused on cultural competency and effective communication.

## Strategies for Fostering Diversity and Innovation

Sage employed several strategies to create a diverse and innovative team. First, he established partnerships with organizations that promote diversity in tech, such as Code2040 and Black Girls Code. These partnerships not only provided access to a wider talent pool but also reinforced Mindful Tech Solutions' commitment to ethical innovation.

Second, Sage fostered an inclusive company culture by implementing policies that promote equity and inclusion. This included flexible work arrangements, mentorship programs, and diversity training. By creating an environment where all team members felt valued and heard, Sage encouraged open dialogue and collaboration, which are essential for innovation.

Moreover, Sage emphasized the importance of interdisciplinary collaboration. By bringing together individuals with expertise in various fields—such as psychology, education, and environmental science—Mindful Tech Solutions was able to approach problems from multiple angles. This interdisciplinary approach led to innovative solutions, such as the redesign of social media platforms to enhance mental well-being, which required insights from both technology and psychology.

## Examples of Successful Diverse Teams

Numerous case studies highlight the success of diverse teams in the tech industry. For instance, the team behind Google's Project Aristotle found that psychological safety—an environment where team members feel safe to take risks and express their ideas—was a key factor in high-performing teams. This finding underscores the importance of fostering a supportive atmosphere where diverse perspectives can thrive.

Similarly, a report by McKinsey & Company (2020) revealed that companies with diverse executive teams are 25% more likely to outperform their peers in terms of profitability. This correlation between diversity and performance reinforces the notion that diverse teams are not only ethically sound but also strategically advantageous.

## Conclusion

In conclusion, assembling a diverse and innovative team is a cornerstone of Sage Yamamoto's vision for Mindful Tech Solutions. By leveraging the theoretical frameworks of social identity and cognitive diversity, addressing the challenges of unconscious bias and team integration, and implementing strategic initiatives to promote inclusivity, Sage was able to create a dynamic team capable of driving ethical innovation. The success of Mindful Tech Solutions serves as a testament to the power of diversity in fostering creativity and developing solutions that resonate with a broad audience. As the tech industry continues to evolve, the lessons learned from Sage's experience will remain relevant, highlighting the need for a commitment to diversity and ethical responsibility in all technological advancements.

## Developing a Company Culture of Ethical Innovation

In the rapidly evolving landscape of technology, cultivating a company culture that prioritizes ethical innovation is not merely an option but a necessity. Sage Yamamoto understood this imperative when founding Mindful Tech Solutions. This section delves into the strategies and frameworks employed by Yamamoto to foster an environment where ethical considerations are at the forefront of innovation.

### Theoretical Frameworks

To establish a culture of ethical innovation, it is essential to ground practices in established theories. One relevant framework is the **Triple Bottom Line** (TBL) approach, which emphasizes the importance of social, environmental, and economic responsibilities. According to Elkington (1997), businesses should evaluate their success not just by profit but also by their impact on people and the planet. This holistic view aligns with Yamamoto's vision, where ethical innovation is seen as a pathway to sustainable success.

### Core Values and Mission Statement

At the heart of any ethical culture lies a clear set of core values. Mindful Tech Solutions implemented a mission statement that encapsulates its commitment to ethical innovation. The mission emphasizes integrity, transparency, and the well-being of users as fundamental principles. By embedding these values into the company's DNA, employees are consistently reminded of their ethical responsibilities. This approach resonates with the **Social Contract Theory**, which posits that organizations must act in the best interests of society to maintain legitimacy and trust (Hobbes, Locke, Rousseau).

### Inclusive Decision-Making

Sage Yamamoto recognized that diverse perspectives lead to more ethical outcomes. To this end, Mindful Tech Solutions adopted an **inclusive decision-making** process. This involves engaging employees from various backgrounds and departments in discussions about ethical dilemmas and innovation strategies. According to research by Page (2007), diversity enhances problem-solving and creativity, which are crucial for ethical innovation. By creating cross-functional teams, the company encourages open dialogue and collective responsibility for ethical outcomes.

## Training and Development Programs

To reinforce a culture of ethical innovation, Mindful Tech Solutions implemented comprehensive training and development programs. These programs focus on ethical decision-making frameworks, such as the **Utilitarian Approach**, which advocates for actions that maximize overall happiness, and the **Deontological Approach**, which emphasizes duty and adherence to rules. Employees engage in workshops that simulate ethical dilemmas, allowing them to practice navigating complex situations. This experiential learning reinforces the idea that ethical considerations are integral to the innovation process.

## Encouraging Whistleblowing and Feedback

Creating a safe environment for employees to voice concerns is crucial for maintaining ethical standards. Mindful Tech Solutions established a robust whistleblower policy that protects individuals who report unethical behavior. This policy is grounded in the **Ethical Climate Theory**, which suggests that organizations with a positive ethical climate encourage reporting and transparency (Victor & Cullen, 1988). Additionally, regular feedback sessions allow employees to express their thoughts on the company's ethical practices and suggest improvements.

## Measuring Ethical Performance

To ensure accountability, Mindful Tech Solutions adopted metrics to measure ethical performance. These metrics include employee satisfaction surveys, stakeholder feedback, and assessments of the social impact of innovations. By regularly evaluating these indicators, the company can identify areas for improvement and celebrate successes. This aligns with the **Balanced Scorecard** approach, which integrates financial and non-financial performance measures to provide a comprehensive view of organizational health (Kaplan & Norton, 1992).

## Real-World Examples

One notable example of ethical innovation at Mindful Tech Solutions is the redesign of their social media platform to prioritize user well-being. By incorporating features that promote digital mindfulness—such as usage reminders and content moderation tools—the company demonstrated its commitment to ethical considerations in product development. This initiative not only enhanced user experience but also positioned the company as a leader in responsible tech.

Another example is the collaboration with local educational institutions to develop ethical tech curricula. By engaging with students and educators, Mindful Tech Solutions fosters a culture of ethical awareness among the next generation of innovators, further solidifying its commitment to ethical innovation.

## Conclusion

In conclusion, developing a company culture of ethical innovation requires a multifaceted approach that integrates theoretical frameworks, core values, inclusive practices, training, and accountability measures. Sage Yamamoto's leadership at Mindful Tech Solutions exemplifies how a commitment to ethics can drive innovation while fostering a positive impact on society. As the tech industry continues to evolve, the importance of cultivating such a culture will only grow, making it essential for future innovators to prioritize ethical considerations in their work.

## Overcoming Startup Challenges and Building Momentum

Starting a tech company, especially one centered on ethical innovation, presents a unique set of challenges that can test the resolve of any entrepreneur. Sage Yamamoto, in her journey to establish Mindful Tech Solutions, faced numerous obstacles that required innovative thinking, resilience, and a steadfast commitment to her vision.

## Identifying Common Startup Challenges

The landscape of tech startups is often marked by uncertainty and high stakes. Some common challenges include:

- **Funding:** Securing initial capital is one of the primary hurdles. Investors often prioritize quick returns, which can conflict with the ethical focus of a mindful tech startup.

- **Market Competition:** The tech industry is saturated with competitors, many of whom are entrenched giants with substantial resources. Gaining traction in such an environment requires differentiation and strategic positioning.

- **Talent Acquisition:** Attracting skilled individuals who share a commitment to ethical innovation can be difficult, especially when larger companies can offer more attractive compensation packages.

- **User Adoption:** Convincing users to switch from established platforms to new, ethically-oriented alternatives can be challenging, particularly in a market driven by convenience and familiarity.

## Building Momentum

To overcome these challenges, Sage employed several strategies that not only helped her startup survive but also thrive in its early stages.

**1. Cultivating a Strong Value Proposition**  Sage understood that in order to attract both investors and users, she needed to articulate a clear value proposition that differentiated Mindful Tech Solutions from its competitors. She emphasized the importance of ethical practices in technology, framing her startup as a solution to the growing concerns over privacy, mental health, and the social implications of tech. This approach not only attracted like-minded individuals but also resonated with a growing consumer base that values ethical consumption.

**2. Leveraging Community Support**  Sage actively engaged with local communities and organizations that shared her vision. By participating in tech meetups, conferences, and panels focused on ethical innovation, she built a network of supporters and potential collaborators. This grassroots approach helped her to garner interest and support for her startup, creating a sense of community around her mission.

**3. Iterative Development and User Feedback**  To ensure that her products met user needs, Sage adopted an iterative development process. This involved releasing early prototypes and gathering user feedback to refine her offerings. By involving users in the development process, she not only improved her products but also built a loyal customer base that felt invested in the success of Mindful Tech Solutions. This approach aligns with the Lean Startup methodology, which emphasizes rapid iteration and customer validation.

**4. Strategic Partnerships**  Recognizing the importance of collaboration, Sage sought out partnerships with other ethical organizations and tech startups. These partnerships allowed her to share resources, knowledge, and networks, which proved invaluable in overcoming the limitations of a small startup. For instance, a collaboration with a mental health organization enabled her to develop tools that were not only innovative but also backed by research and expertise in the field.

5. **Focusing on Sustainable Growth**   Sage was committed to building a sustainable business model that prioritized long-term growth over short-term gains. This meant making strategic decisions that aligned with her ethical values, even if they did not provide immediate financial returns. For example, she opted to reinvest profits into developing new features that enhanced user well-being, rather than maximizing short-term profits through aggressive marketing tactics.

## Real-World Examples

Several successful ethical tech startups have navigated similar challenges:

- **Patagonia:** While not a tech startup in the traditional sense, Patagonia's commitment to environmental sustainability has garnered a loyal customer base. Their focus on ethical practices has helped them stand out in a competitive retail market, serving as an inspiration for tech startups like Mindful Tech Solutions.
- **Headspace:** This mindfulness app has successfully captured the attention of users by emphasizing mental well-being. Their user-centric approach and partnerships with mental health professionals illustrate the importance of aligning product offerings with user needs.

## Conclusion

Overcoming the challenges of starting a tech company focused on ethical innovation requires a multifaceted approach. By cultivating a strong value proposition, leveraging community support, adopting iterative development, forming strategic partnerships, and focusing on sustainable growth, Sage Yamamoto was able to build momentum for Mindful Tech Solutions. Her journey exemplifies how commitment to ethical principles can not only guide a startup through turbulent waters but can also pave the way for meaningful impact in the tech industry.

## Gaining Traction in the Tech Industry

Sage Yamamoto's journey to establish Mindful Tech Solutions was not merely a matter of creating innovative products; it was about gaining traction in a competitive tech landscape that often prioritized profit over ethical considerations. This section explores the strategies employed by Sage and her team to carve out a niche for themselves in the industry, the challenges they faced, and the theoretical frameworks that guided their approach.

## Understanding Market Dynamics

To gain traction, it was crucial for Sage to understand the dynamics of the tech market. The technology sector is characterized by rapid innovation, shifting consumer preferences, and intense competition. According to the *Diffusion of Innovations Theory* proposed by Rogers (1962), the adoption of new ideas and technologies occurs through a process involving several stages: awareness, interest, evaluation, trial, and adoption. Sage recognized that to achieve widespread adoption of her ethical tech solutions, she needed to navigate these stages effectively.

## Creating a Unique Value Proposition

Sage's first step in gaining traction was to articulate a compelling value proposition that differentiated Mindful Tech Solutions from other startups. The company focused on the intersection of technology and ethics, emphasizing how their products were designed not only to enhance user experience but also to promote mental well-being and social responsibility. This dual focus resonated with a growing segment of consumers who were increasingly concerned about the ethical implications of technology.

$$\text{Value Proposition} = \text{User Experience} + \text{Ethical Impact} \qquad (9)$$

This equation illustrates the balance between user satisfaction and ethical responsibility that Sage aimed to achieve. By leveraging this unique value proposition, Mindful Tech Solutions positioned itself as a leader in the emerging field of mindful technology.

## Building Strategic Partnerships

Gaining traction also required building strategic partnerships with other organizations and stakeholders who shared a commitment to ethical innovation. Sage actively sought collaborations with educational institutions, non-profits, and established tech companies interested in social responsibility. These partnerships not only provided access to resources and expertise but also enhanced the credibility of Mindful Tech Solutions in the eyes of potential customers.

For example, a partnership with a prominent mental health organization allowed Mindful Tech to develop a mindfulness app that integrated therapeutic techniques with technology. This collaboration not only broadened the app's reach but also validated its effectiveness, as it was endorsed by mental health professionals.

## Leveraging Social Media and Community Engagement

In today's digital age, social media serves as a powerful tool for gaining traction. Sage recognized the importance of building a community around Mindful Tech Solutions. The company utilized platforms like Twitter, Instagram, and LinkedIn to engage with users, share insights about ethical technology, and promote their products. By fostering an online community, Sage was able to create a sense of belonging among users who shared similar values.

Moreover, Sage initiated campaigns that encouraged users to share their experiences with Mindful Tech products, creating a grassroots movement that amplified the company's message. This user-generated content acted as social proof, further enhancing the brand's visibility and credibility.

## Navigating Regulatory Challenges

As Mindful Tech Solutions gained traction, Sage faced the inevitable challenge of navigating the regulatory landscape. The tech industry is subject to various laws and regulations concerning data privacy, consumer protection, and ethical standards. Sage understood that compliance with these regulations was not just a legal obligation but also a moral imperative.

To address these challenges, Sage established a dedicated compliance team that worked closely with legal experts to ensure that all products met regulatory requirements. This proactive approach not only minimized legal risks but also built trust with users who valued transparency and ethical practices.

## Measuring Impact and Success

To assess the traction gained in the tech industry, Sage implemented a framework for measuring the impact of Mindful Tech Solutions. This framework included key performance indicators (KPIs) such as user engagement, customer satisfaction, and social impact metrics.

$$\text{Impact} = \text{User Engagement} \times \text{Social Impact Metrics} \qquad (10)$$

This equation emphasizes the dual focus on user engagement and social impact as critical components of success. By continuously measuring and analyzing these metrics, Sage was able to refine her strategies and ensure that Mindful Tech Solutions remained aligned with its mission of ethical innovation.

## Conclusion

Gaining traction in the tech industry was a multifaceted endeavor for Sage Yamamoto and Mindful Tech Solutions. By understanding market dynamics, creating a unique value proposition, building strategic partnerships, leveraging social media, navigating regulatory challenges, and measuring impact, Sage was able to establish her company as a leader in the field of mindful technology. The journey was fraught with challenges, but Sage's commitment to ethical innovation and her ability to adapt to the ever-changing landscape of the tech industry ultimately led to the success of Mindful Tech Solutions.

# Innovations that Matter

## Redesigning Social Media for Mental Well-being

In an era where social media platforms dominate communication and interaction, the implications of their design on mental well-being have garnered significant attention. Sage Yamamoto recognized the urgent need to redesign social media to foster positive mental health outcomes, addressing the detrimental effects often associated with traditional platforms.

## Theoretical Framework

The redesign of social media for mental well-being can be anchored in several psychological theories. One prominent theory is the **Social Comparison Theory**, proposed by Festinger (1954). This theory posits that individuals determine their own social and personal worth based on how they stack up against others, leading to feelings of inadequacy and anxiety when exposed to curated and idealized representations of others' lives on social media.

Another relevant framework is the **Uses and Gratifications Theory**, which suggests that users actively seek out media to fulfill specific needs, including social interaction, information seeking, and entertainment (Katz, Blumler, & Gurevitch,

1973). Understanding these motivations is crucial in redesigning platforms to enhance user experience and satisfaction, ultimately supporting mental health.

## Identifying Problems

The traditional design of social media platforms often exacerbates mental health issues. Key problems include:

- **Addiction and Overuse:** The infinite scroll feature and notification alerts can lead to compulsive usage patterns, contributing to anxiety and depression.
- **Cyberbullying and Harassment:** Many users experience negative interactions online, leading to severe psychological distress.
- **Fear of Missing Out (FOMO):** Constant exposure to friends' activities can lead to feelings of exclusion and loneliness.
- **Unrealistic Standards:** The prevalence of edited images and highlight reels fosters unattainable standards of beauty and success, impacting self-esteem.

## Innovative Solutions

To address these issues, Sage Yamamoto and his team at Mindful Tech Solutions implemented several innovative features aimed at promoting mental well-being:

- **Mindfulness Prompts:** Integrating reminders for users to take breaks, practice mindfulness, and engage in offline activities. For instance, a notification might suggest, "Take a moment to breathe and reflect before scrolling further."
- **Positive Interaction Algorithms:** Redesigning algorithms to prioritize content that fosters positive interactions and connections, rather than sensational or divisive material. This could involve showing users more posts from friends that express gratitude or positivity.
- **Community Support Features:** Creating spaces for users to share mental health challenges and support one another. For example, a dedicated forum for discussing mental health topics, moderated by professionals, can provide a safe space for users.
- **Content Filters:** Allowing users to filter out content that may trigger negative feelings, such as body image issues or comparisons. Users could customize their feeds to minimize exposure to harmful content.

- **Educational Resources:** Providing access to mental health resources, including articles, videos, and helplines, directly within the platform. This could be a section labeled "Mental Health Resources" that users can easily access.

### Case Study: Mindful Connect

One of the successful implementations of these principles is the platform **Mindful Connect**, developed by Yamamoto's team. This platform was designed with user well-being at its core. Key features included:

- **Gratitude Sharing:** Users are encouraged to share daily gratitude posts, fostering a culture of positivity and appreciation.
- **Wellness Check-Ins:** Regular prompts for users to assess their mental state and connect with friends for support.
- **Community Challenges:** Initiatives such as "30 Days of Kindness" that encourage users to engage in positive actions both online and offline.

The impact of Mindful Connect has been significant, with user surveys indicating a 40% increase in reported feelings of connection and a 30% reduction in feelings of anxiety related to social media use.

### Conclusion

Redesigning social media for mental well-being is a critical step toward creating healthier digital environments. By leveraging psychological theories and addressing existing problems, innovators like Sage Yamamoto can transform social media from a source of stress to a platform that promotes mental health and well-being. The success of initiatives like Mindful Connect serves as a beacon of hope for the future of social media, illustrating that ethical innovation can lead to positive societal change.

## Introduction of Mindfulness Tech Tools

In an era where technology often exacerbates stress and anxiety, the introduction of mindfulness tech tools represents a transformative shift in how individuals engage with digital platforms. These tools are designed to promote mental well-being, enhance focus, and foster a deeper connection with oneself and the environment. This section explores the theoretical foundations, challenges, and practical examples of mindfulness tech tools developed under Sage Yamamoto's vision of ethical innovation.

## Theoretical Foundations

Mindfulness, rooted in ancient contemplative practices, emphasizes present-moment awareness and acceptance. Research in psychology, particularly the works of Jon Kabat-Zinn, has established that mindfulness can significantly reduce stress and improve emotional regulation. The integration of mindfulness into technology draws on various theories, including:

- **Cognitive Behavioral Theory (CBT):** This theory posits that our thoughts influence our emotions and behaviors. Mindfulness tech tools often incorporate CBT principles to help users identify negative thought patterns and replace them with positive ones.

- **Self-Determination Theory (SDT):** This theory emphasizes the importance of autonomy, competence, and relatedness in fostering motivation. Mindfulness tools encourage users to take control of their mental health, enhancing their sense of agency.

- **Flow Theory:** Proposed by Mihaly Csikszentmihalyi, flow theory describes a state of complete immersion and engagement in an activity. Mindfulness tools aim to facilitate flow experiences by minimizing distractions and promoting focused attention.

## Identifying Problems Addressed by Mindfulness Tech Tools

Despite the growing prevalence of technology, many individuals experience heightened levels of stress and anxiety. The following problems highlight the need for mindfulness tech tools:

- **Digital Overload:** With constant notifications and information bombardment, individuals often feel overwhelmed. Mindfulness tools provide strategies to manage digital consumption and encourage intentional engagement.

- **Mental Health Crisis:** The rise in mental health issues, particularly among younger demographics, necessitates accessible solutions. Mindfulness tech tools offer scalable interventions that can be utilized anytime and anywhere.

# INNOVATIONS THAT MATTER

- **Lack of Awareness and Connection**: Many individuals struggle to maintain a connection with themselves and their surroundings. Mindfulness tools foster self-awareness and promote a sense of presence in daily life.

## Examples of Mindfulness Tech Tools

Sage Yamamoto's company, Mindful Tech Solutions, has pioneered several mindfulness tech tools that embody ethical innovation. Below are notable examples:

- **Mindful Moments App**: This mobile application encourages users to take short mindfulness breaks throughout the day. It utilizes reminders and guided meditations to help users cultivate awareness and reduce stress. Research indicates that even brief mindfulness practices can lead to significant improvements in emotional well-being [?].

- **FocusFlow Browser Extension**: Designed to combat digital distractions, this browser extension provides users with customizable focus sessions. It blocks distracting websites and incorporates mindfulness prompts to help users remain present during work or study periods. A study by Mark et al. (2018) found that minimizing distractions can enhance productivity and overall satisfaction.

- **Mindful Learning Platform**: This educational platform integrates mindfulness practices into learning environments. It offers courses that teach students how to apply mindfulness techniques to enhance focus, retention, and emotional regulation. Evidence suggests that mindfulness training can lead to improved academic performance and emotional resilience [?].

- **Virtual Reality Mindfulness Experiences**: Utilizing VR technology, these immersive experiences transport users to calming environments, facilitating deep relaxation and mindfulness. Research has shown that VR can effectively induce relaxation and reduce anxiety levels [?].

## Challenges and Ethical Considerations

While the introduction of mindfulness tech tools offers numerous benefits, several challenges and ethical considerations must be addressed:

- **Accessibility**: Ensuring that mindfulness tech tools are accessible to diverse populations is crucial. This includes considering socioeconomic factors, digital literacy, and language barriers.

- **Data Privacy**: As mindfulness tools often collect user data to personalize experiences, safeguarding this information is paramount. Ethical considerations surrounding data usage and user consent must be prioritized to maintain trust.

- **Commercialization vs. Authenticity**: The commercialization of mindfulness can dilute its essence. It is essential to strike a balance between providing valuable tools and maintaining the integrity of mindfulness practices.

In conclusion, the introduction of mindfulness tech tools represents a significant advancement in promoting mental well-being in our technology-driven world. By addressing the challenges of digital overload and mental health crises, these tools embody Sage Yamamoto's vision of ethical innovation. As we move forward, it is imperative to navigate the ethical landscape surrounding these tools to ensure they fulfill their potential in fostering a more mindful and connected society.

## Transforming the Education System with Ethical Tech

The education system is at a pivotal crossroads, where the integration of technology can either enhance learning or exacerbate existing inequalities. Sage Yamamoto's commitment to ethical innovation has led to transformative approaches in educational technology, focusing on accessibility, inclusivity, and mental well-being. This section explores how ethical tech can revolutionize education, the challenges it faces, and real-world examples of its implementation.

### The Need for Ethical Tech in Education

The traditional education system often perpetuates disparities, with marginalized groups facing barriers to quality education. According to the *OECD Education at a Glance* report, students from low-income families are significantly less likely to have access to advanced coursework and technology compared to their affluent peers [1]. This disparity calls for a shift towards ethical tech solutions that prioritize equity and inclusivity.

## Principles of Ethical Tech in Education

1. **Accessibility**: Ethical tech should ensure that all students, regardless of socioeconomic status or ability, have equal access to educational resources. This involves designing platforms that accommodate diverse learning needs, such as dyslexia-friendly interfaces or multilingual support.

2. **Data Privacy**: With the rise of digital learning tools, concerns about data privacy have escalated. Ethical tech in education must prioritize the protection of student data, adhering to regulations such as the Family Educational Rights and Privacy Act (FERPA) in the U.S. [2].

3. **Mental Well-being**: The impact of technology on mental health is a growing concern. Ethical tech should promote positive interactions and discourage harmful behaviors, such as cyberbullying. Integrating mindfulness practices into educational platforms can help foster a supportive learning environment.

## Innovative Examples of Ethical Tech in Education

1. **Adaptive Learning Technologies**   Adaptive learning platforms, such as *Knewton* and *DreamBox*, utilize algorithms to personalize educational experiences based on individual student performance. These platforms analyze data to identify learning gaps and adapt content accordingly, ensuring that each student receives tailored support. This approach not only enhances learning outcomes but also reduces the risk of students falling behind.

2. **Open Educational Resources (OER)**   OER initiatives, such as the *OpenStax* project, provide free, high-quality educational materials to students and educators worldwide. By removing financial barriers, OER promotes equitable access to quality education. Furthermore, these resources can be modified and shared, fostering collaboration among educators and encouraging innovative teaching practices.

3. **Mindfulness and Social-Emotional Learning (SEL) Tools**   Platforms like *Calm Classroom* and *Headspace for Kids* incorporate mindfulness techniques into the educational experience. These tools help students manage stress, improve focus, and enhance emotional regulation. By prioritizing mental well-being, these applications contribute to a healthier learning environment, ultimately leading to better academic performance.

## Challenges in Implementing Ethical Tech in Education

Despite the potential benefits, several challenges hinder the widespread adoption of ethical tech in education:

1. **Resistance to Change**  Educators and institutions may resist adopting new technologies due to a lack of training or fear of the unknown. To overcome this barrier, comprehensive professional development programs must be established, equipping educators with the skills needed to effectively integrate ethical tech into their classrooms.

2. **Funding and Resources**  Many schools, particularly those in low-income areas, struggle to secure funding for technological advancements. Collaborative efforts between governments, private sectors, and non-profit organizations are essential to provide the necessary resources for implementing ethical tech solutions.

3. **Ensuring Quality and Effectiveness**  Not all educational technologies are created equal. Rigorous evaluation processes must be established to assess the effectiveness of tech tools in enhancing learning outcomes. This includes gathering feedback from educators, students, and parents to ensure that the technology meets their needs.

## Conclusion

Sage Yamamoto's vision for transforming the education system through ethical tech highlights the importance of creating inclusive, accessible, and supportive learning environments. By addressing the challenges and implementing innovative solutions, we can pave the way for a future where technology serves as a powerful ally in education, fostering a generation of learners equipped to thrive in an ever-evolving world.

# Bibliography

[1] OECD (2020). *Education at a Glance 2020: OECD Indicators*. OECD Publishing, Paris.

[2] Family Educational Rights and Privacy Act (FERPA). (2021). U.S. Department of Education.

## Revolutionizing Healthcare with Mindful Tech Solutions

The intersection of technology and healthcare has historically been marked by rapid advancements and innovative solutions. However, the integration of mindful tech solutions into healthcare represents a paradigm shift, focusing not just on efficiency and profit but on the holistic well-being of patients. This section explores how Sage Yamamoto's Mindful Tech Solutions are revolutionizing healthcare by addressing critical issues such as patient engagement, mental health, and data privacy.

## The Need for Mindful Innovations in Healthcare

Healthcare systems globally face numerous challenges, including rising costs, fragmented care, and patient dissatisfaction. According to a report by the World Health Organization (WHO), approximately 400 million people lack access to essential health services, highlighting the urgent need for innovative solutions. Furthermore, mental health issues are on the rise, with the WHO estimating that depression will be the leading cause of disability by 2030. This landscape necessitates a shift towards mindful tech solutions that prioritize ethical considerations and patient-centered care.

## Key Innovations by Mindful Tech Solutions

1. **Telehealth Platforms for Accessibility**  One of the flagship innovations of Mindful Tech Solutions is the development of telehealth platforms that enhance

accessibility for patients. These platforms utilize video conferencing and AI-driven chatbots to provide remote consultations, significantly reducing the barriers to healthcare access. A case study involving a rural community in the Midwest demonstrated that telehealth services increased patient engagement by 60% and reduced no-show rates by 30%. By leveraging technology, Sage Yamamoto's team has made healthcare more accessible to underserved populations.

2. **Mental Health Apps for Well-being** Mindful Tech Solutions has also introduced mental health applications designed to support users in managing stress, anxiety, and depression. These apps incorporate cognitive behavioral therapy (CBT) principles and mindfulness techniques, providing users with tools to enhance their mental well-being. For instance, the app "CalmMind" includes features such as guided meditations, mood tracking, and personalized wellness plans. Research published in the Journal of Medical Internet Research shows that users of such apps reported a 40% reduction in anxiety symptoms over a three-month period.

3. **Data Privacy and Ethical Considerations** In an era where data breaches are commonplace, Mindful Tech Solutions emphasizes the importance of data privacy in healthcare technology. The company adheres to strict ethical guidelines and employs advanced encryption techniques to protect sensitive patient information. By implementing a user-centric data policy, patients are empowered to control their own data, fostering trust and transparency. The ethical framework guiding these innovations is rooted in the principles of beneficence and non-maleficence, ensuring that technology serves the best interests of patients.

## Challenges and Solutions

Despite the promising advancements, the integration of mindful tech solutions in healthcare is not without challenges. One significant hurdle is the resistance from traditional healthcare providers who may be hesitant to adopt new technologies. To address this, Mindful Tech Solutions has initiated partnerships with healthcare organizations to provide training and resources, ensuring that providers are equipped to utilize these tools effectively.

Another challenge is the digital divide, where disparities in technology access can exacerbate health inequalities. To combat this, the company has launched initiatives aimed at providing free or low-cost devices and internet access to low-income communities, thereby promoting equitable healthcare access.

## Case Studies of Impact

Several case studies illustrate the transformative impact of mindful tech solutions in healthcare. In a pilot program conducted in partnership with a local hospital, Mindful Tech Solutions implemented a digital platform for chronic disease management. Patients using the platform showed a 25% improvement in adherence to treatment plans compared to those receiving traditional care. This success prompted the hospital to adopt the platform as a standard practice, showcasing how mindful tech can lead to better health outcomes.

Additionally, a collaboration with a mental health clinic resulted in the creation of a community support app that connects users with peer support groups. The app facilitated over 1,000 connections within the first month of launch, demonstrating the power of technology in fostering community and support for mental health issues.

## Conclusion

Sage Yamamoto's Mindful Tech Solutions is at the forefront of revolutionizing healthcare through ethical and mindful innovations. By addressing accessibility, mental health, and data privacy, the company is not only improving patient outcomes but also setting new standards for ethical practices in the healthcare technology industry. As we look to the future, the integration of mindful tech solutions will play a crucial role in shaping a more equitable, compassionate, and efficient healthcare system.

## The Impact of Mindful Tech on Environmental Sustainability

In an era where climate change and environmental degradation have reached critical levels, the intersection of technology and sustainability has become a focal point for innovators. Mindful Tech, as pioneered by Sage Yamamoto, emphasizes ethical practices that not only foster technological advancement but also prioritize the health of our planet. This section explores the profound impact of Mindful Tech on environmental sustainability, highlighting relevant theories, challenges, and successful implementations.

### Theoretical Framework

The concept of *Sustainable Development* serves as a foundational theory for understanding the role of Mindful Tech in promoting environmental sustainability. According to the Brundtland Report (1987), sustainable development is defined as "development that meets the needs of the present without compromising the ability of future generations to meet their own needs." Mindful Tech aligns with this principle by integrating environmental considerations into technology design and implementation.

Moreover, the *Circular Economy* model is critical in this context, advocating for a system where resources are reused, recycled, and repurposed. This model contrasts with the traditional linear economy, which follows a "take-make-dispose" pattern. Mindful Tech leverages innovations that facilitate circularity, thereby reducing waste and minimizing the environmental footprint.

## Challenges in Environmental Sustainability

Despite the potential benefits, several challenges hinder the integration of Mindful Tech in promoting environmental sustainability:

- **Resource Intensity:** Many tech solutions require significant resources for production and operation. For instance, the manufacturing of electronic devices often involves rare minerals, leading to ecological disruption and resource depletion.

- **E-Waste Management:** The rapid turnover of technology contributes to the growing problem of electronic waste (e-waste), which poses severe environmental hazards if not managed properly.

- **Greenwashing:** Some companies may engage in misleading practices, promoting products as environmentally friendly without substantial evidence. This undermines genuine efforts toward sustainability.

## Mindful Tech Innovations in Environmental Sustainability

Sage Yamamoto's Mindful Tech Solutions have pioneered several innovations that address these challenges:

- **Eco-Friendly Product Design:** By adopting principles of sustainable design, companies can create products that are easier to recycle and made from biodegradable materials. For example, the use of plant-based plastics in consumer electronics significantly reduces reliance on fossil fuels.

- **Smart Resource Management:** Technologies such as the Internet of Things (IoT) enable smarter resource management. For instance, smart grids optimize energy use, reducing waste and improving efficiency. A study by the *International Energy Agency* (IEA) found that smart grid technologies could reduce energy consumption by up to 15%.

- **Carbon Footprint Tracking:** Mindful Tech applications help individuals and organizations track their carbon footprints, promoting awareness and encouraging sustainable practices. An example is the app *Carbon Footprint Tracker*, which allows users to monitor their daily emissions and provides suggestions for reduction.

- **Sustainable Agriculture Technologies:** Innovations such as precision farming use data analytics and IoT to optimize resource use in agriculture, leading to reduced water consumption and minimized pesticide usage. A case study of a California farm using precision agriculture techniques reported a 20% reduction in water use while maintaining crop yield.

## Case Studies and Examples

Several organizations exemplify the successful application of Mindful Tech in promoting environmental sustainability:

- **Patagonia:** This outdoor clothing brand integrates environmental sustainability into its business model by using recycled materials and promoting fair labor practices. Their *Worn Wear* program encourages customers to repair and recycle their clothing, embodying the principles of the circular economy.

- **Tesla:** By focusing on electric vehicles and renewable energy solutions, Tesla has significantly contributed to reducing greenhouse gas emissions in the transportation sector. The company's commitment to sustainability is evident in its goal to produce battery technology that minimizes environmental impact.

- **Ecovative Design:** This company utilizes mycelium, the root structure of mushrooms, to create sustainable packaging materials that decompose naturally, offering a viable alternative to plastic packaging.

## Conclusion

The impact of Mindful Tech on environmental sustainability is profound and multifaceted. By integrating ethical considerations into technological advancements, innovators like Sage Yamamoto are paving the way for a future where technology not only serves human needs but also respects and nurtures the planet. As we face escalating environmental challenges, the principles of Mindful Tech will be essential in guiding the development of sustainable solutions that ensure the well-being of future generations. The journey toward a more sustainable world requires continuous innovation, collaboration, and a commitment to ethical practices that prioritize the health of our planet.

# Chapter Three: Navigating Challenges

## Facing Obstacles and Criticism

### Ethical Dilemmas in a Rapidly Advancing Tech Landscape

The rapid advancement of technology presents a myriad of ethical dilemmas that challenge innovators like Sage Yamamoto. As technology evolves, it often outpaces the frameworks designed to govern its use, leading to complex situations where the right course of action is not always clear. This section explores several key ethical dilemmas that arise in this context, supported by relevant theories and examples.

### The Dilemma of Privacy

One of the foremost ethical dilemmas in the tech landscape is the issue of privacy. With the proliferation of data collection technologies, individuals are often unaware of how their personal information is being used. The theory of *informed consent* posits that individuals should have the right to know what data is collected and how it is used. However, many tech companies operate under opaque data policies, making it difficult for users to give informed consent.

For instance, consider the case of social media platforms that utilize algorithms to target ads based on user behavior. Users may not fully understand that their interactions are being tracked and analyzed, leading to a breach of their privacy. This raises the question: *To what extent should companies prioritize user privacy over their business interests?*

## Algorithmic Bias

Another significant ethical dilemma arises from algorithmic bias. Algorithms, while designed to be objective, can inadvertently perpetuate existing societal biases. This phenomenon is often explained through the lens of *social constructivism*, which suggests that technology is influenced by the social contexts in which it is developed.

For example, a well-documented case involves facial recognition technology, which has been shown to misidentify individuals of certain racial and ethnic backgrounds at higher rates than others. A study by the MIT Media Lab found that facial recognition systems misclassified the gender of darker-skinned women with an error rate of 34.7%, compared to just 0.8% for lighter-skinned men. This raises ethical questions about the responsibility of tech companies to ensure their products do not reinforce harmful stereotypes or discrimination.

## The Impact of Automation on Employment

Automation and artificial intelligence (AI) are transforming industries at an unprecedented rate, leading to concerns about job displacement. The *utilitarianism* ethical theory, which advocates for actions that maximize overall happiness, is often invoked in debates about automation. Proponents argue that automation can lead to increased efficiency and economic growth, benefiting society as a whole. However, this overlooks the immediate suffering of those who lose their jobs.

For instance, in the manufacturing sector, robots have replaced many assembly line workers, leading to significant unemployment in certain regions. The ethical dilemma here is whether the benefits of automation justify the harm caused to individuals and communities. Should companies be held accountable for the social consequences of their innovations?

## The Responsibility of Tech Companies

As technology becomes increasingly integrated into daily life, the question of corporate responsibility emerges. The theory of *corporate social responsibility* (CSR) argues that businesses have an obligation to act in ways that benefit society, beyond merely generating profit. This raises the dilemma of how tech companies can balance their profit motives with their ethical responsibilities.

For example, consider the case of a tech company that develops a new app that enhances productivity but also encourages overwork and burnout. While the app may be profitable, it raises ethical concerns about its impact on users' mental health.

The dilemma lies in whether the company should prioritize user well-being over financial gain.

## The Ethics of Surveillance Technology

The rise of surveillance technology presents another ethical challenge. Governments and corporations increasingly use surveillance tools to monitor individuals, often justified by the need for security. However, this leads to a conflict between the right to privacy and the perceived need for safety, a classic case of the *social contract* theory.

For instance, the implementation of facial recognition cameras in public spaces has sparked debates about the balance between public safety and individual privacy rights. Critics argue that such surveillance can lead to a chilling effect on free speech and assembly, as individuals may feel less inclined to express dissenting opinions if they know they are being watched.

## Conclusion

In conclusion, the ethical dilemmas in a rapidly advancing tech landscape are multifaceted and complex. Innovators like Sage Yamamoto must navigate these challenges by prioritizing ethical considerations in their decision-making processes. As technology continues to evolve, it is imperative that ethical frameworks evolve alongside it to ensure that innovation serves the greater good, rather than exacerbating existing societal issues. The future of mindful tech relies on a commitment to addressing these dilemmas head-on, fostering a landscape where technology enhances rather than undermines human dignity and societal well-being.

## Overcoming Resistance from Industry Giants

Sage Yamamoto's journey in establishing Mindful Tech Solutions was not without its challenges, particularly in overcoming significant resistance from established industry giants. These powerful entities often possess extensive resources, market dominance, and entrenched interests that can stifle innovation, especially when it threatens their business models. This section explores the strategies employed by Yamamoto to navigate this treacherous landscape.

## Understanding the Landscape

The technology sector is characterized by a few dominant players who control large portions of the market. According to the *Market Concentration Theory*, high levels of concentration can lead to anti-competitive behaviors, including predatory pricing and aggressive lobbying against emerging competitors. Yamamoto recognized that these industry giants would likely view his ethical innovations as a threat to their profit margins.

## Building a Unique Value Proposition

To counteract this resistance, Yamamoto focused on developing a compelling value proposition that differentiated Mindful Tech Solutions from the incumbents. By emphasizing the societal benefits of ethical technology, he positioned his startup as not just a competitor, but a necessary evolution in the tech landscape. This approach was grounded in the *Diffusion of Innovations Theory*, which posits that innovations are adopted based on perceived advantages, compatibility, complexity, trialability, and observability.

$$\text{Adoption Rate} = f(\text{Perceived Advantage, Compatibility, Complexity}) \quad (11)$$

Yamamoto's innovations, such as redesigning social media platforms to promote mental well-being, were framed as not only ethical but also beneficial for user engagement and satisfaction, thus appealing to both consumers and investors.

## Leveraging Alliances and Collaborations

Recognizing the power of collective action, Yamamoto sought alliances with other ethical innovators and organizations. This strategic collaboration not only amplified his voice but also created a network of support that could counterbalance the influence of larger corporations. For instance, partnerships with educational institutions allowed for joint research initiatives that validated the effectiveness of mindful tech solutions, providing empirical evidence against the skepticism often posed by industry giants.

## Navigating Legal and Regulatory Challenges

Industry giants often wield significant influence over regulatory frameworks, which can be a formidable barrier for startups. Yamamoto adopted a proactive approach by engaging with policymakers to advocate for regulations that promote ethical practices in technology. By participating in public forums and contributing to policy discussions, he positioned himself as a thought leader in the ethical tech space, gaining credibility and visibility.

## Utilizing Public Sentiment and Consumer Advocacy

Public sentiment plays a crucial role in shaping the landscape of technology adoption. As consumers became increasingly aware of the ethical implications of their digital interactions, Yamamoto harnessed this momentum by launching awareness campaigns that highlighted the negative impacts of traditional tech practices. By engaging directly with consumers through social media and grassroots movements, he cultivated a loyal customer base that demanded more ethical options, thus applying pressure on industry giants to adapt or risk losing market share.

## Case Study: The Battle Against Data Privacy Violations

One notable instance of resistance came when Mindful Tech Solutions launched a campaign against data privacy violations perpetuated by larger social media platforms. Yamamoto's team developed a comprehensive report showcasing the detrimental effects of data misuse on mental health and societal well-being. This report not only garnered media attention but also sparked discussions among consumers and policymakers, leading to increased scrutiny of the practices employed by industry giants.

## Conclusion

Overcoming resistance from industry giants required a multifaceted strategy that combined innovative thinking, strategic alliances, legal advocacy, and public engagement. Sage Yamamoto's ability to navigate these challenges exemplifies the resilience and adaptability required for ethical innovation in a competitive landscape. By positioning Mindful Tech Solutions as a leader in ethical practices, he not only disrupted the status quo but also paved the way for a more conscientious approach to technology that prioritizes human well-being over profit.

## Navigating Legal and Regulatory Hurdles

In the fast-evolving landscape of technology, navigating the legal and regulatory environment is a critical challenge for innovators like Sage Yamamoto. As technology advances, so too do the laws and regulations that govern its use, often struggling to keep pace with the rapid changes. This section explores the complexities of legal compliance, the challenges faced by ethical innovators, and the strategies employed to overcome these hurdles.

## The Complexity of Technology Law

The legal framework surrounding technology is multifaceted, encompassing various domains such as intellectual property, data privacy, cybersecurity, and consumer protection. For instance, the General Data Protection Regulation (GDPR) in Europe has set stringent guidelines on data collection and processing, requiring companies to implement robust data protection measures. Failing to comply with such regulations can result in hefty fines, legal action, and reputational damage.

$$F = m \cdot a \qquad (12)$$

Where $F$ is the force exerted by legal compliance, $m$ is the mass of the regulations, and $a$ is the acceleration of technological advancement. As the mass of regulations increases, the force required to comply also grows, creating a significant burden for startups.

## Intellectual Property Challenges

Innovators like Sage must also navigate the complexities of intellectual property (IP) law. Protecting proprietary technology while ensuring that it does not infringe on existing patents is a delicate balancing act. For example, when developing new mindfulness tech tools, Sage's team needed to conduct thorough patent searches and possibly engage in licensing negotiations to avoid litigation. This process can be time-consuming and expensive, diverting resources from innovation to legal compliance.

## Data Privacy and User Consent

Data privacy is another significant hurdle. With increasing scrutiny on how companies handle user data, ethical innovators must prioritize transparency and user consent. Sage's approach involved implementing clear privacy policies and obtaining informed consent from users. This not only helped in complying with regulations but also built trust with users, reinforcing the company's commitment to ethical practices.

## Regulatory Compliance Strategies

To successfully navigate these legal and regulatory hurdles, Sage Yamamoto adopted several strategies:

- **Engaging Legal Expertise:** Sage assembled a team of legal experts specializing in technology law to provide ongoing guidance. This proactive approach ensured that the company remained compliant with evolving regulations.

- **Continuous Education:** Sage emphasized the importance of continuous education for her team regarding legal obligations. Regular training sessions on data protection laws and ethical standards were implemented to foster a culture of compliance.

- **Collaboration with Regulators:** Building relationships with regulatory bodies allowed Sage to stay ahead of potential changes in the law. By participating in industry forums and discussions, her team could provide input on emerging regulations, ensuring that their perspectives as ethical innovators were considered.

## Case Study: Mindful Tech Solutions

A practical example of navigating these hurdles can be seen in the case of Mindful Tech Solutions, where Sage faced a significant regulatory challenge while launching a new social media platform designed to promote mental well-being. The platform's features included user-generated content, which raised concerns about data privacy and user safety.

To address these concerns, Sage's team implemented a multi-layered approach:

- **User Safety Features:** They introduced robust content moderation tools and reporting mechanisms to ensure a safe environment for users. This proactive measure not only complied with legal requirements but also enhanced user trust.

- **Transparent Data Policies:** The company published clear and accessible data policies that outlined how user data would be collected, stored, and used. This transparency helped mitigate potential legal risks and fostered user engagement.

- **Feedback Mechanisms:** Sage's team established feedback loops with users to continuously improve the platform based on user experiences and concerns, ensuring that the platform remained compliant and user-friendly.

## Conclusion

Navigating legal and regulatory hurdles is an ongoing challenge for ethical innovators like Sage Yamamoto. By adopting proactive strategies, engaging legal experts, and fostering a culture of compliance, Sage was able to not only overcome these challenges but also set a precedent for other innovators in the tech industry. The lessons learned from her journey underscore the importance of integrating legal considerations into the innovation process, ultimately contributing to a more ethical and responsible tech landscape.

## Addressing Privacy Concerns and Protecting User Data

In an era where data is often referred to as the new oil, the ethical management of user data has emerged as a critical concern for innovators in technology. Sage Yamamoto, through his venture Mindful Tech Solutions, recognized early on that the integrity of user data was paramount not only for compliance with legal frameworks but also for building trust with users. This section explores the challenges associated with privacy concerns and the strategies employed by Yamamoto to protect user data.

### Theoretical Framework

Privacy concerns in technology can be analyzed through various theoretical lenses, including the *Social Contract Theory* and *Privacy Calculus Theory*. The Social Contract Theory posits that individuals consent, either explicitly or implicitly, to surrender some degree of privacy in exchange for certain benefits, such as personalized services. However, when organizations fail to uphold their end of the bargain, they breach this social contract, leading to distrust and potential backlash.

On the other hand, Privacy Calculus Theory suggests that users weigh the benefits of sharing their data against the potential risks of privacy loss. This evaluation often leads to a reluctance to share personal information, especially when users perceive that companies prioritize profit over ethical considerations.

### Challenges in Protecting User Data

The rapid advancement of technology has introduced several challenges in protecting user data, including:

- **Data Breaches:** High-profile data breaches, such as the Equifax incident in 2017, have exposed the sensitive information of millions, highlighting the vulnerability of even the most established companies. These breaches not only compromise user privacy but can also lead to identity theft and financial loss.

- **Inadequate Regulations:** The regulatory landscape surrounding data privacy is often fragmented and inconsistent. For example, while the General Data Protection Regulation (GDPR) in Europe sets a high standard for data protection, many countries lack similar regulations, creating a patchwork of compliance challenges for global companies.

- **User Awareness:** A significant challenge is the general lack of awareness among users regarding their data rights. Many individuals do not fully understand how their data is collected, used, and shared, leading to a sense of helplessness and mistrust.

## Strategies Implemented by Sage Yamamoto

To address these challenges, Sage Yamamoto implemented several key strategies within Mindful Tech Solutions:

- **Transparent Data Practices:** Yamamoto emphasized transparency in data collection and usage. Users are informed about what data is collected, how it will be used, and with whom it may be shared. This transparency fosters trust and aligns with the principles of the Social Contract Theory.

- **User-Controlled Privacy Settings:** Mindful Tech Solutions developed user-friendly interfaces that allow individuals to easily manage their privacy settings. Users can opt-in or opt-out of data collection processes, providing them with a sense of control over their personal information.

- **Robust Security Measures:** To mitigate the risk of data breaches, the company invested in advanced cybersecurity measures, including encryption, multi-factor authentication, and regular security audits. By prioritizing security, Mindful Tech Solutions aims to protect user data proactively.

- **Education and Advocacy:** Recognizing the importance of user awareness, Yamamoto initiated educational campaigns to inform users about their data rights and the implications of data sharing. Collaborating with organizations focused on digital literacy, Mindful Tech Solutions sought to empower users to make informed decisions regarding their privacy.

- **Ethical Data Use Policies:** The company adopted a strict ethical framework that governs data usage. This framework ensures that user data is only utilized for purposes that align with user consent and societal benefit, thus adhering to the principles of ethical innovation.

## Case Study: Mindful Social Media Platform

One of the flagship products developed by Mindful Tech Solutions was a social media platform designed with user privacy at its core. Unlike traditional platforms that monetize user data through targeted advertising, this platform operated on a subscription model, allowing users to pay for services without compromising their privacy.

The platform employed a unique algorithm that prioritized user well-being over engagement metrics, thereby reducing the pressure to share personal information. For instance, users could engage with content without the fear of their data being harvested for advertising purposes. This approach not only protected user data but also fostered a healthier online environment.

## Conclusion

Addressing privacy concerns and protecting user data is not merely a regulatory obligation but a moral imperative for innovators in technology. Sage Yamamoto's commitment to ethical practices in data management exemplifies how mindful innovation can lead to a more trustworthy tech landscape. As technology continues to evolve, the principles of transparency, user control, and ethical responsibility will remain crucial in safeguarding user privacy and fostering a culture of trust in the digital age.

# Balancing Profitability and Ethical Practices

In today's rapidly evolving technological landscape, the challenge of balancing profitability with ethical practices has become a central concern for innovators like Sage Yamamoto. The intersection of ethics and business profitability is not merely a theoretical debate; it is a practical issue that affects how companies operate, how they are perceived by the public, and ultimately, their long-term sustainability.

## Theoretical Framework

To understand the dynamics of balancing profitability and ethical practices, we can refer to several key theories in business ethics:

- **Stakeholder Theory:** This theory posits that companies should consider the interests of all stakeholders, not just shareholders. By prioritizing ethical practices, companies can build trust and loyalty among customers, employees, and the community, which can lead to enhanced profitability in the long run.

- **Triple Bottom Line:** This framework emphasizes the importance of balancing social, environmental, and economic responsibilities. Organizations that adopt this approach recognize that ethical practices can contribute to sustainable profitability by reducing risks associated with social and environmental issues.

- **Corporate Social Responsibility (CSR):** CSR emphasizes the role of businesses in contributing positively to society. Companies that engage in CSR initiatives often find that their ethical commitments resonate with consumers, leading to increased brand loyalty and market share.

## Challenges in Balancing Profitability and Ethics

Despite the theoretical underpinnings supporting ethical business practices, numerous challenges arise in the pursuit of this balance:

- **Short-Term vs. Long-Term Goals:** Many companies face pressure to deliver immediate financial results, which can lead to compromises in ethical standards. For instance, a tech startup might prioritize rapid growth and revenue generation over developing products that prioritize user privacy and data protection.

- **Market Competition:** In highly competitive markets, businesses may feel compelled to adopt aggressive strategies that could undermine ethical practices. For example, a company might engage in misleading advertising or exploit labor in order to reduce costs and increase profit margins.

- **Consumer Expectations:** While consumers increasingly demand ethical practices, their purchasing behavior often contradicts this expectation. For instance, consumers may express a preference for sustainable products but still choose cheaper, less ethical alternatives when making purchasing decisions.

## Examples of Successful Balancing Acts

Sage Yamamoto's journey exemplifies how ethical innovation can coincide with profitability. Through Mindful Tech Solutions, Yamamoto has implemented several strategies that demonstrate this balance:

- **User-Centric Design:** By prioritizing user well-being in product design, Mindful Tech Solutions has created social media platforms that promote mental health. This approach not only fulfills ethical obligations but also attracts a loyal user base, resulting in increased advertising revenue.

- **Transparent Practices:** The company's commitment to transparency regarding data usage has fostered trust among users. This trust translates into a competitive advantage, as consumers are more likely to engage with brands that prioritize their privacy.

- **Community Engagement:** Mindful Tech Solutions invests in community initiatives that promote digital literacy and ethical tech usage. These initiatives not only enhance the company's reputation but also expand its market reach, leading to increased profitability.

## Quantitative Analysis of Profitability and Ethics

To quantitatively assess the relationship between ethical practices and profitability, we can consider the following equation:

$$P = R - C \tag{13}$$

Where:

- $P$ = Profit

- $R$ = Revenue generated from ethical practices

- $C$ = Costs associated with ethical compliance

In this equation, it is crucial to recognize that while the initial costs of implementing ethical practices (C) may be high, the long-term revenue (R) generated from increased customer loyalty and brand reputation can far outweigh these costs, leading to sustainable profitability.

## Conclusion

In conclusion, balancing profitability and ethical practices is a complex but essential endeavor for modern innovators like Sage Yamamoto. By embracing stakeholder theory, the triple bottom line, and corporate social responsibility, companies can navigate the challenges of ethical business while still achieving financial success. The examples set forth by Mindful Tech Solutions illustrate that ethical innovation is not just a moral imperative but a viable pathway to long-term profitability. As the tech industry continues to evolve, the call for a more mindful approach to business will only grow louder, urging innovators to find harmony between profit and principle.

# Impact and Recognition

## Changing Lives with Mindful Tech Solutions

In the rapidly evolving landscape of technology, the introduction of mindful tech solutions has become a beacon of hope for individuals and communities seeking to navigate the complexities of modern life. Sage Yamamoto's approach to ethical innovation has not only transformed industries but has also had a profound impact on the lives of everyday people. This section explores how mindful tech solutions are changing lives, addressing both theoretical frameworks and practical applications.

## Theoretical Frameworks

Mindful technology can be understood through the lens of several key theories that emphasize the relationship between technology, well-being, and ethical considerations. One such framework is the **Technology Acceptance Model (TAM)** which posits that perceived ease of use and perceived usefulness significantly influence users' decisions to embrace new technologies [?]. In the context of mindful tech, these principles are adapted to ensure that technology not only serves functional purposes but also enhances mental and emotional well-being.

Additionally, the concept of **Digital Well-Being** has emerged, focusing on how technology can be designed to promote healthier interactions and reduce negative impacts on mental health. This theory posits that technology should be a tool for empowerment rather than a source of stress or anxiety [?]. By integrating these frameworks into the design and implementation of tech solutions, Sage Yamamoto and his team have created products that resonate with users on a deeper level.

## Practical Applications

One of the most significant contributions of mindful tech solutions is in the realm of mental health. For instance, the development of **MindfulSocial**, a reimagined social media platform, exemplifies how technology can prioritize mental well-being. Unlike traditional platforms that often foster comparison and anxiety, MindfulSocial employs algorithms designed to encourage positive interactions and reduce exposure to harmful content. Users report feeling more connected and less anxious, demonstrating the platform's effectiveness in changing lives for the better.

$$\text{User Well-Being} = f(\text{Positive Interactions, Reduced Exposure to Negative Content}) \tag{14}$$

This equation highlights the relationship between user well-being and the key factors that MindfulSocial manipulates to enhance user experience. By focusing on positive interactions and minimizing exposure to negativity, the platform creates a supportive community that fosters mental health.

Another notable innovation is the introduction of **MindfulTech Tools**—a suite of applications designed to help users incorporate mindfulness practices into their daily routines. These tools include guided meditation sessions, breathing exercises, and reminders to take mindful breaks throughout the day. Research has shown that regular mindfulness practice can lead to significant improvements in stress management, emotional regulation, and overall quality of life [?].

$$\text{Stress Reduction} = g(\text{Frequency of Mindfulness Practice, Duration of Practice}) \tag{15}$$

This equation illustrates the correlation between the frequency and duration of mindfulness practice and the resulting stress reduction. Users of MindfulTech Tools have reported a marked decrease in stress levels, showcasing the practical impact of these innovations.

In the educational sector, Sage Yamamoto's initiatives have transformed the learning experience for students. The introduction of **EthicalEdTech**, a platform that integrates ethical considerations into educational technology, has empowered educators to create more inclusive and supportive learning environments. By providing resources that promote critical thinking about technology's role in society, EthicalEdTech encourages students to become responsible digital citizens.

## Case Studies

To illustrate the impact of mindful tech solutions, consider the case of a high school student named Emily. Struggling with anxiety and the pressures of social media, Emily found solace in MindfulSocial. After joining the platform, she experienced a significant reduction in her anxiety levels, stating, "I feel like I can be myself without the fear of judgment." This anecdote highlights how mindful tech can create safe spaces for individuals, ultimately changing lives for the better.

Another compelling example is the use of MindfulTech Tools in a corporate setting. A tech company implemented these tools to support employee well-being, resulting in a 30% decrease in reported stress levels and a 20% increase in productivity over six months. Employees noted that the tools helped them manage their workloads more effectively and fostered a healthier work-life balance.

## Conclusion

The impact of mindful tech solutions, as pioneered by Sage Yamamoto, extends far beyond the realm of technology itself. By prioritizing ethical considerations and user well-being, these innovations are changing lives, fostering healthier relationships with technology, and promoting a culture of mindfulness. As the world continues to grapple with the challenges posed by rapid technological advancement, the lessons learned from these mindful tech solutions will be crucial in shaping a more ethical and compassionate future.

## Awards and Accolades for Ethical Innovation

Sage Yamamoto's journey in the realm of Mindful Tech not only revolutionized the industry but also garnered significant recognition for ethical innovation. These awards and accolades serve as both validation of his efforts and a beacon for other innovators aspiring to integrate ethics into technology.

### The Importance of Recognition

Recognition in the form of awards can amplify the impact of ethical innovation by:

- **Raising Awareness:** Awards draw public attention to ethical issues in technology, encouraging discourse among stakeholders.
- **Setting Standards:** Recognized innovators often set benchmarks for ethical practices within their industries.

- **Inspiring Future Innovators:** Awards highlight successful models of ethical innovation, motivating the next generation to pursue similar paths.

## Major Awards Received by Sage Yamamoto

Throughout his career, Sage received numerous awards that underscored his commitment to ethical innovation:

- **The Tech for Good Award (2025):** This prestigious award recognized companies that leverage technology to create a positive social impact. Yamamoto's startup was honored for its innovative approach to redesigning social media platforms to promote mental well-being, addressing issues such as cyberbullying and addiction.

- **Global Ethical Innovation Award (2026):** This award is given to individuals or organizations that demonstrate outstanding ethical practices in technology. Sage was lauded for his contributions to the field of healthcare technology, specifically for developing tools that prioritize patient privacy and informed consent.

- **The Mindful Leadership Award (2027):** This accolade is awarded to leaders who exemplify mindfulness in their business practices. Yamamoto's emphasis on a collaborative and inclusive company culture earned him this recognition, showcasing his commitment to ethical leadership.

- **Environmental Innovation Prize (2028):** Sage's initiatives in promoting sustainability through technology were recognized with this award. His efforts to integrate eco-friendly practices into tech solutions helped reduce the carbon footprint of his startup.

## Impact of Awards on Sage's Work

The accolades received by Sage Yamamoto had a profound impact on both his work and the broader tech community.

- **Increased Visibility:** Awards provided a platform for Sage to share his vision of ethical innovation, allowing him to reach a wider audience and influence industry standards.

- **Networking Opportunities:** Recognition opened doors to collaborations with other ethical innovators and organizations, fostering a community dedicated to responsible tech development.

- **Funding and Support:** Accolades often attracted investors and partners who were interested in supporting ethical initiatives, enabling Sage to expand his projects and influence.

## Challenges in Ethical Recognition

Despite the accolades, Sage faced challenges in the recognition of ethical innovation:

- **Skepticism from Industry Peers:** Some industry leaders questioned the feasibility of ethical practices, viewing them as potential barriers to profitability. Sage often had to defend his approach, emphasizing that ethical innovation could lead to long-term success.

- **Balancing Recognition and Responsibility:** As awards increased, so did the expectations. Sage had to ensure that his company maintained its ethical standards while navigating the pressures of growth and recognition.

- **Navigating Bias in Award Selection:** The criteria for awards can sometimes favor established companies over startups, leading to a lack of diversity in recognized innovators. Sage advocated for more inclusive award processes to highlight a broader range of contributions to ethical tech.

## Conclusion

Sage Yamamoto's accolades for ethical innovation underscore the importance of integrating ethical considerations into technology. His journey illustrates that recognition not only validates the work of innovators but also serves as a catalyst for change within the industry. As the tech landscape continues to evolve, the lessons learned from Sage's experiences can guide future innovators in their pursuit of ethical advancements, ensuring that technology remains a force for good in society.

Through these awards, Sage has not only solidified his legacy but has also inspired a movement towards a more mindful and ethical approach to technology, encouraging others to follow in his footsteps.

## Influencing the Tech Industry's Approach to Ethics

Sage Yamamoto's journey in the realm of mindful technology has not only transformed her own company but has also significantly influenced the broader tech industry's approach to ethics. This influence can be observed through a variety of mechanisms, including the establishment of ethical frameworks, advocacy for regulatory changes, and the promotion of transparency in tech practices.

## Establishing Ethical Frameworks

One of the primary ways Sage has impacted the tech industry is through the development of comprehensive ethical frameworks that guide technological innovation. These frameworks emphasize the importance of considering the societal implications of technology from the outset. For instance, the **Ethical Design Principles** proposed by Yamamoto include:

- **User-Centric Design:** Prioritizing user well-being and mental health in the design process.

- **Transparency:** Ensuring that users are aware of how their data is being used and the implications of technology on their lives.

- **Accountability:** Holding companies responsible for the consequences of their technological innovations.

These principles have been adopted by several startups and established companies alike, leading to a shift in how technology is conceptualized and created.

## Advocacy for Regulatory Changes

In addition to establishing ethical frameworks, Sage has been a vocal advocate for regulatory changes that promote ethical practices within the tech industry. Recognizing the rapid pace of technological advancement, she has called for the creation of regulatory bodies that can oversee ethical compliance in technology development. For example, her advocacy led to the proposal of a **Tech Ethics Oversight Committee** (TEOC), which would be responsible for reviewing new technologies and assessing their ethical implications before they reach the market.

This committee would employ a framework similar to the **Precautionary Principle**, which states that in the absence of scientific consensus, the burden of proof falls on those advocating for an activity that may cause harm to the public or the environment. By applying this principle to technology, companies would be required to demonstrate that their innovations do not pose undue risks to society.

## Promoting Transparency

Transparency has become a cornerstone of Sage's influence in the tech industry. She has championed initiatives that require companies to disclose their data practices and the algorithms that drive their technologies. This push for transparency is critical in an era where data privacy concerns are at an all-time high. For instance, the implementation of the **Transparency in Algorithms Act** proposed by Yamamoto aims to:

- Require companies to publish the criteria and data sets used in algorithmic decision-making.

- Mandate independent audits of algorithms to ensure they are free from bias and discrimination.

- Establish a public repository of algorithmic models that can be accessed and scrutinized by researchers and the public.

By advocating for these measures, Sage has encouraged a culture of openness that empowers users and fosters trust between technology companies and their customers.

## Case Studies of Influence

Several case studies illustrate the significant impact of Sage's efforts on the tech industry:

**Case Study 1: Social Media Redesign** A prominent social media platform, influenced by Yamamoto's ethical design principles, underwent a major redesign focused on user well-being. The company implemented features that limit screen time and promote positive interactions. As a result, user engagement metrics improved, and the platform reported a decrease in mental health-related complaints from users.

**Case Study 2: Healthcare Technology** In the healthcare sector, a startup adopted Yamamoto's frameworks to create an app that prioritizes patient privacy and informed consent. The app includes features that allow patients to control their data and understand how it is being used. This approach not only improved patient trust but also positioned the startup as a leader in ethical healthcare technology.

## Conclusion

Sage Yamamoto's influence on the tech industry's approach to ethics is profound and multifaceted. By establishing ethical frameworks, advocating for regulatory changes, and promoting transparency, she has set a new standard for how technology is developed and implemented. Her initiatives have not only reshaped individual companies but have also contributed to a broader cultural shift towards ethical responsibility in technology. As the industry continues to evolve, the principles championed by Yamamoto will likely serve as a guiding light for future innovations, ensuring that technology serves humanity rather than undermines it.

## Fostered Organizational Culture of Ethical Responsibility

Sage Yamamoto recognized that for Mindful Tech Solutions to truly embody ethical innovation, it was essential to cultivate an organizational culture that prioritized ethical responsibility at every level. This culture not only influenced internal practices but also set a standard for the entire tech industry. The foundation of this culture was built upon several key theoretical frameworks and practical applications.

### Theoretical Frameworks

One of the primary theories that guided the development of this ethical culture was the **Stakeholder Theory**. According to Freeman (1984), businesses should create value for all stakeholders involved, not just shareholders. This perspective encourages companies to consider the impacts of their decisions on employees, customers, suppliers, and the community. In practice, this meant that Mindful Tech Solutions engaged in regular stakeholder consultations, ensuring that diverse voices were heard and integrated into decision-making processes.

Another relevant framework was **Corporate Social Responsibility (CSR)**, which posits that companies have an obligation to act ethically and contribute positively to society. Yamamoto's approach to CSR was not merely a marketing tactic; it was embedded in the company's mission. For instance, the company initiated projects aimed at improving digital literacy in underserved communities, thus aligning their business objectives with social good.

### Challenges in Fostering an Ethical Culture

While the vision was clear, implementing an ethical organizational culture was fraught with challenges. One significant issue was the **conflict of interest** that often arises in tech companies. Employees might feel pressured to prioritize profit over ethical considerations, especially in a competitive industry. To counter this, Yamamoto instituted a comprehensive **ethics training program** that included real-world scenarios and role-playing exercises. This training emphasized the importance of ethical decision-making and equipped employees with the tools to navigate dilemmas they might encounter.

Additionally, the company faced the challenge of **employee buy-in**. Not all team members initially embraced the ethical culture, leading to resistance in some quarters. To address this, Yamamoto implemented a system of **transparent communication**. Regular town hall meetings were held to discuss ethical challenges the company faced, successes achieved, and the importance of maintaining ethical standards. This transparency fostered a sense of ownership among employees, as they felt their contributions were valued and their concerns addressed.

## Practical Applications and Examples

To further solidify this culture, Mindful Tech Solutions adopted several practical measures. One notable initiative was the establishment of an **Ethics Committee**, composed of employees from various departments. This committee was tasked with reviewing company policies and practices to ensure they aligned with ethical standards. For instance, when developing new features for their social media platform, the committee evaluated potential impacts on user mental health, ensuring that design choices promoted well-being rather than addiction.

Moreover, the company instituted a **whistleblower policy** that encouraged employees to report unethical behavior without fear of retaliation. This policy was critical in fostering an environment where ethical concerns could be raised openly. For example, when a developer discovered a potential data privacy issue, they felt empowered to report it, leading to swift action that mitigated a significant risk.

## Impact on the Tech Industry

The commitment to fostering an organizational culture of ethical responsibility had a ripple effect beyond Mindful Tech Solutions. As the company gained recognition for its ethical practices, other tech firms began to take notice. Yamamoto was invited to speak at industry conferences, where he shared insights on building an ethical culture. His advocacy for transparency and stakeholder engagement became a blueprint for other organizations seeking to enhance their ethical standards.

Furthermore, the success of Mindful Tech Solutions demonstrated that ethical practices could coexist with profitability. The company's growth trajectory, driven by its commitment to ethical innovation, challenged the prevailing notion that profit maximization necessitated compromising ethical values. This shift in perspective encouraged a broader movement within the tech industry towards integrating ethical considerations into business strategies.

## Conclusion

In conclusion, Sage Yamamoto's efforts to foster an organizational culture of ethical responsibility at Mindful Tech Solutions exemplify the potential for ethical innovation to transform the tech industry. By embedding ethical principles into the company's DNA, addressing challenges head-on, and leading by example, Yamamoto not only shaped his organization but also influenced the broader landscape of technology. This commitment to ethics serves as a reminder that responsible innovation is not just possible, but essential for sustainable success in the digital age.

## Collaboration with Other Ethical Innovators

Sage Yamamoto understood that the journey toward ethical innovation was not a solitary endeavor; it required collaboration and synergy among like-minded individuals and organizations. This section delves into the significance of collaboration in fostering ethical practices within the tech industry, highlighting key partnerships, frameworks, and outcomes that emerged from these collaborative efforts.

### The Value of Collaboration

Collaboration among ethical innovators is crucial for several reasons:

- **Diverse Perspectives:** Bringing together individuals from different backgrounds and disciplines fosters a rich tapestry of ideas. This diversity enhances problem-solving capabilities and leads to more robust ethical frameworks.

- **Resource Sharing:** Collaboration allows for the pooling of resources, knowledge, and skills. By working together, innovators can leverage each other's strengths to develop solutions that are not only innovative but also ethically sound.

- **Increased Impact:** Collective efforts amplify the reach and effectiveness of initiatives aimed at promoting ethical technology. By joining forces, innovators can create a larger impact than they could achieve alone.

## Frameworks for Collaboration

To effectively collaborate, Sage and his peers established frameworks that guided their partnerships:

1. **Ethical Innovation Networks (EINs):** These networks comprised startups, academic institutions, and non-profit organizations committed to ethical technology. By sharing best practices and research, EINs fostered an environment conducive to innovation.

2. **Joint Research Initiatives:** Sage partnered with universities to conduct research on the ethical implications of emerging technologies. This collaboration not only advanced academic inquiry but also ensured that ethical considerations were integrated into technological development from the outset.

3. **Collaborative Workshops and Conferences:** Sage organized events that brought together ethical innovators to share insights, discuss challenges, and brainstorm solutions. These gatherings served as incubators for new ideas and collaborations.

## Examples of Successful Collaborations

**Case Study: The Mindful Tech Alliance** One of the most notable collaborations was the formation of the Mindful Tech Alliance (MTA), a coalition of startups and ethical organizations dedicated to promoting mindfulness in technology. The MTA focused on:

- Developing guidelines for ethical AI usage.
- Creating tools to measure the impact of technology on mental health.
- Advocating for policies that prioritize user well-being over profit.

Through the MTA, Sage and his collaborators successfully launched a series of mindfulness applications that integrated ethical considerations into their design. These applications received widespread acclaim for their positive impact on mental health, showcasing the power of collaboration in achieving meaningful outcomes.

**Case Study: Partnership with Educational Institutions** Sage also recognized the importance of education in fostering a culture of ethical innovation. He collaborated with educational institutions to develop curricula focused on ethics in technology. This partnership led to:

- The creation of interdisciplinary courses that combined computer science, ethics, and social responsibility.

- Initiatives that encouraged students to engage in ethical hackathons, where they could apply their skills to solve real-world problems.

- Scholarships for underrepresented students pursuing careers in ethical technology.

These educational initiatives not only empowered the next generation of innovators but also ensured that ethical considerations became a foundational aspect of technological development.

## Challenges in Collaboration

Despite the many benefits of collaboration, Sage encountered several challenges:

- **Differing Objectives:** Collaborators often had varying goals, which could lead to conflicts. Sage emphasized the importance of aligning objectives and establishing clear communication channels to mitigate misunderstandings.

- **Resource Disparities:** Not all partners had equal access to resources, which could create imbalances in contributions. Sage advocated for equitable resource distribution to ensure all voices were heard.

- **Navigating Bureaucracy:** Collaborating with larger organizations sometimes involved navigating complex bureaucratic structures, which could slow down progress. Sage learned to be patient and persistent, focusing on building relationships to facilitate smoother collaboration.

## Conclusion

Sage Yamamoto's commitment to collaboration with other ethical innovators exemplified the belief that collective action is essential for driving meaningful change in the tech industry. By leveraging diverse perspectives, sharing resources, and overcoming challenges, these collaborations not only advanced ethical innovation but also inspired a new generation of thinkers dedicated to creating a more mindful and responsible technological landscape. As the tech industry continues to evolve, the importance of collaboration among ethical innovators remains paramount in ensuring that technology serves humanity rather than the other way around.

$$\text{Impact} = \text{Innovation} \times \text{Collaboration} \tag{16}$$

This equation encapsulates the essence of Sage's philosophy: the greater the collaboration, the more significant the impact of ethical innovations on society.

# Chapter Four: Beyond Business

## Philanthropy and Social Responsibility

### Investing in Sustainable Technologies

In the contemporary landscape of technological advancement, the emphasis on sustainability has become paramount. As we grapple with the consequences of climate change, resource depletion, and social inequities, innovators like Sage Yamamoto recognize that investing in sustainable technologies is not merely a choice but a necessity for ensuring the well-being of future generations. This section explores the rationale behind such investments, the challenges faced, and notable examples that highlight the efficacy of sustainable technology initiatives.

### The Rationale for Sustainable Investment

The rationale for investing in sustainable technologies can be viewed through various lenses: environmental, economic, and ethical.

**Environmental Perspective**   From an environmental standpoint, the adoption of sustainable technologies aims to reduce the carbon footprint and mitigate the adverse effects of climate change. According to the Intergovernmental Panel on Climate Change (IPCC), global greenhouse gas emissions must be reduced by approximately 45% by 2030 to limit global warming to 1.5 degrees Celsius above pre-industrial levels [?].   Sustainable technologies such as renewable energy systems, energy-efficient appliances, and sustainable agriculture practices contribute significantly to this reduction.

**Economic Perspective**   Economically, sustainable technologies can drive innovation and create new markets. The global market for clean energy is projected to reach $2.15 trillion by 2025 [?]. Investing in these technologies not only fosters economic growth but also enhances energy security and reduces dependency on fossil fuels, which are subject to volatile price fluctuations.

**Ethical Perspective**    Ethically, there is a growing recognition of the responsibility that businesses and innovators have towards society. As articulated by the United Nations Sustainable Development Goals (SDGs), there is a clear mandate to promote sustainable practices that address poverty, inequality, and environmental degradation. By investing in sustainable technologies, innovators like Sage Yamamoto align their ventures with these global objectives, reinforcing their commitment to ethical leadership.

## Challenges in Sustainable Investment

Despite the clear benefits, investing in sustainable technologies is fraught with challenges:

**High Initial Costs**    One of the primary barriers to the adoption of sustainable technologies is the high initial investment required. For instance, while solar panels can lead to significant long-term savings on energy bills, their upfront costs can be prohibitive for many individuals and businesses. This phenomenon is often referred to as the "green premium," where sustainable options are more expensive than conventional alternatives [?].

**Technological Uncertainty**    Another challenge is the uncertainty surrounding the efficacy and reliability of emerging technologies. For example, while electric vehicles (EVs) present a sustainable alternative to traditional vehicles, concerns regarding battery life, charging infrastructure, and range anxiety can hinder widespread adoption.

**Regulatory Hurdles**    Regulatory frameworks can also pose challenges. Inconsistent policies and lack of incentives for sustainable practices can stymie innovation. Innovators often find themselves navigating a complex landscape of regulations that can vary significantly by region, complicating efforts to scale sustainable technologies.

## Notable Examples of Sustainable Technologies

Despite these challenges, several successful examples illustrate the potential of sustainable technology investments:

**Tesla, Inc.**   Tesla has emerged as a leader in sustainable transportation through its production of electric vehicles and energy storage solutions. The company's commitment to sustainability is evident in its Gigafactories, which aim to produce batteries at scale while minimizing environmental impact. By leveraging economies of scale, Tesla has significantly reduced the cost of battery production, making EVs more accessible to consumers.

**Solar Power Innovations**   Companies like First Solar have pioneered the development of thin-film solar panels that are both cost-effective and efficient. These innovations have made solar energy more accessible and have contributed to a substantial increase in solar installations worldwide. According to the Solar Energy Industries Association (SEIA), the U.S. solar market grew by 167% from 2010 to 2020 [?], showcasing the potential for sustainable technologies to disrupt traditional energy markets.

**Vertical Farming**   Vertical farming represents another innovative approach to sustainability in agriculture. By utilizing controlled environments and hydroponics, companies like AeroFarms are able to grow crops with significantly less water and land than traditional farming methods. This technology not only addresses food security concerns but also reduces the carbon footprint associated with transporting food over long distances.

## Conclusion

In conclusion, investing in sustainable technologies is essential for fostering a more resilient and equitable future. While challenges such as high initial costs and regulatory hurdles persist, the potential benefits—environmental sustainability, economic growth, and ethical responsibility—far outweigh these obstacles. Innovators like Sage Yamamoto exemplify the transformative power of sustainable investments, paving the way for a greener, more mindful technological landscape. As we move forward, it is imperative that stakeholders across sectors collaborate to create an ecosystem that supports and accelerates the development and adoption of sustainable technologies.

## Supporting Ethical Initiatives Worldwide

Sage Yamamoto's commitment to ethical technology extends beyond the confines of his own startup, *Mindful Tech Solutions*. Recognizing that the challenges posed by rapid technological advancements are global in nature, Sage has made it a priority to support ethical initiatives worldwide. This section explores the various ways in which he has contributed to fostering ethical practices in technology across different regions and sectors.

## Global Collaborations

One of the most effective strategies Sage employed was forming partnerships with international organizations that share a commitment to ethical technology. Collaborating with groups such as *Tech for Good* and *The Ethical Tech Alliance*, Sage helped create a platform for sharing best practices and resources. These collaborations have facilitated the exchange of ideas and strategies among innovators from diverse backgrounds, leading to the development of culturally sensitive ethical frameworks.

For instance, during a summit in Amsterdam, Sage presented a case study on the impact of algorithmic bias in social media platforms. His insights prompted discussions on how to develop algorithms that are not only efficient but also fair and inclusive. Such dialogues have been instrumental in shaping policies that prioritize ethical considerations in technology development.

## Funding Ethical Initiatives

Sage has also taken a proactive approach to funding ethical initiatives worldwide. Through the *Sage Yamamoto Foundation*, he has provided financial support to grassroots organizations that focus on technology education, digital rights, and ethical innovation. By investing in these initiatives, Sage aims to empower communities to harness technology responsibly.

For example, in collaboration with *Digital Rights Watch*, the foundation funded a project aimed at educating marginalized communities about their digital rights. This initiative not only raised awareness but also equipped individuals with the knowledge to advocate for their rights in the digital space. Such efforts highlight the importance of community engagement in fostering a culture of ethical technology.

## Promoting Ethical Standards

In addition to funding and collaboration, Sage has been a vocal advocate for establishing global ethical standards in technology. He has actively participated in international forums, such as the *Global Summit on Technology Ethics*, where he has called for the creation of a universal code of ethics for technology developers. This code would address issues such as data privacy, algorithmic transparency, and user consent.

The proposed framework emphasizes the need for accountability and responsibility among tech companies. For instance, Sage argues that companies should be required to conduct impact assessments before launching new technologies. These assessments would evaluate potential ethical implications, ensuring that innovations do not inadvertently harm society.

## Case Studies of Impact

Several case studies illustrate the success of Sage's efforts in supporting ethical initiatives. In one notable instance, a partnership with a nonprofit organization in India led to the development of a mobile application designed to promote digital literacy among rural populations. The app, which was created with input from local communities, emphasizes ethical usage of technology and encourages users to think critically about the information they consume.

Another example is Sage's involvement in a project focused on sustainable technology in Africa. By supporting solar energy startups, Sage has helped communities reduce their reliance on fossil fuels while promoting ethical business practices. These initiatives demonstrate the potential for technology to drive social change when guided by ethical considerations.

## Challenges and Solutions

Despite the successes, supporting ethical initiatives worldwide is not without challenges. One major issue is the disparity in resources between developed and developing regions. Many grassroots organizations lack the funding and expertise needed to implement ethical practices effectively. To address this, Sage has advocated for a model of shared resources, where established tech companies provide mentorship and support to smaller organizations.

Moreover, the rapidly evolving nature of technology presents another challenge. Ethical considerations can quickly become outdated as new technologies emerge. To combat this, Sage emphasizes the importance of continuous education and adaptation. He promotes the idea that ethical frameworks should be living documents, regularly updated to reflect the latest advancements and societal needs.

## Conclusion

Sage Yamamoto's commitment to supporting ethical initiatives worldwide exemplifies his vision for a more responsible tech industry. Through global collaborations, funding, advocacy for ethical standards, and addressing challenges, he has made significant strides in promoting ethical practices in technology. As the tech landscape continues to evolve, Sage's efforts serve as a reminder of the importance of prioritizing ethics in innovation, ensuring that technology serves humanity as a whole.

In summary, the integration of ethical considerations into technology development is not merely a local concern but a global imperative. Sage's work highlights the interconnectedness of our world and the collective responsibility we share in shaping a future where technology enhances, rather than diminishes, the human experience.

## Using Wealth for Positive Change

In the realm of ethical innovation, the responsible use of wealth becomes a powerful tool for driving social change. Sage Yamamoto exemplifies how financial resources can be harnessed to address pressing global issues, thereby creating a ripple effect that extends beyond individual success. This section explores the theories and practical applications of using wealth for positive change, highlighting the challenges and triumphs faced by innovators like Yamamoto.

### Theoretical Framework

The concept of using wealth for positive change is grounded in several theoretical perspectives, including philanthropy, social entrepreneurship, and corporate social responsibility (CSR). Philanthropy involves the donation of money, resources, or time to support charitable causes, while social entrepreneurship focuses on creating sustainable solutions to social problems through innovative business models. CSR emphasizes the ethical obligations of businesses to contribute positively to society while pursuing profit.

One relevant theory is the **Stakeholder Theory**, which posits that businesses should consider the interests of all stakeholders, including employees, customers, suppliers, and the community, rather than solely focusing on shareholders. This approach encourages companies to use their wealth to benefit society, fostering a more equitable and sustainable world.

### Challenges in Philanthropic Efforts

Despite the noble intentions behind using wealth for positive change, several challenges can hinder these efforts:

- **Allocation of Resources:** Determining the most effective way to allocate funds can be complex. There is often a tension between supporting immediate needs (e.g., disaster relief) and investing in long-term solutions (e.g., education and infrastructure).

- **Impact Measurement:** Evaluating the effectiveness of philanthropic initiatives can be difficult. Metrics for success may vary, and quantifying social impact often requires sophisticated methodologies.

- **Dependency Issues:** There is a risk that well-intentioned financial support may create dependency rather than fostering self-sufficiency within communities.

- **Public Perception:** Philanthropists may face scrutiny regarding their motives, with critics arguing that their wealth could be better utilized through systemic changes rather than charitable giving.

## Examples of Positive Change

Sage Yamamoto's approach to philanthropy illustrates how wealth can be effectively utilized to create positive change. Through the establishment of the **Sage Yamamoto Foundation**, he has focused on several key initiatives:

- **Educational Programs:** The foundation has invested in educational programs aimed at underrepresented communities, providing scholarships, mentorship, and resources to empower the next generation of innovators. For example, the foundation launched the *Tech for All* initiative, which offers coding boot camps and workshops in underserved neighborhoods.

- **Sustainable Technologies:** Recognizing the urgent need for environmental sustainability, Yamamoto has funded projects that develop renewable energy solutions and promote sustainable agricultural practices. His support for the *Green Tech Challenge* has spurred innovation in clean energy technologies, leading to the creation of affordable solar panels for low-income households.

- **Mental Health Initiatives:** Understanding the importance of mental well-being in the digital age, the foundation has partnered with mental health organizations to create awareness campaigns and provide resources for those in need. The *Mindfulness Matters* program offers workshops and online resources to promote mental health awareness in schools and workplaces.

## The Ripple Effect of Wealth Utilization

The impact of using wealth for positive change extends beyond immediate beneficiaries. By investing in ethical initiatives, innovators like Yamamoto inspire others to follow suit, creating a culture of giving and social responsibility. This ripple effect can lead to a collective movement towards a more equitable society.

$$\text{Social Impact} = \text{Investment} \times \text{Community Engagement} \qquad (17)$$

This equation highlights the relationship between financial investment and the level of community engagement in driving social impact. The more engaged a community is, the greater the potential for transformative change.

## Conclusion

Sage Yamamoto's commitment to using wealth for positive change serves as a model for future innovators. By strategically allocating resources to address pressing social issues, he exemplifies the potential of ethical innovation to create lasting impacts. As more individuals and organizations embrace this approach, the landscape of philanthropy and social entrepreneurship will continue to evolve, paving the way for a more sustainable and just world.

## Creating Opportunities for Underrepresented Communities

In the quest for a more equitable tech industry, Sage Yamamoto's initiatives have focused on creating opportunities for underrepresented communities, recognizing that diversity is not just a moral imperative but a business necessity. The tech sector has long been criticized for its lack of representation, particularly among women, people of color, and those from lower socioeconomic backgrounds. This section explores the strategies employed by Sage and Mindful Tech Solutions to address these disparities and promote inclusivity.

### The Importance of Diversity in Tech

Research has consistently shown that diverse teams outperform their homogeneous counterparts. According to a study by McKinsey [?], companies in the top quartile for gender diversity on executive teams were 21% more likely to experience above-average profitability. Furthermore, teams that are ethnically diverse are 33% more likely to outperform their peers [?]. This correlation highlights the need for intentional efforts to include voices from different backgrounds in the tech industry.

## Barriers to Entry

Despite the clear benefits of diversity, several barriers prevent underrepresented groups from entering the tech field. These include:

- **Educational Disparities:** Many individuals from marginalized communities lack access to quality education and resources necessary to pursue careers in technology.

- **Economic Barriers:** The high cost of education and training programs can be prohibitive for those from low-income backgrounds.

- **Bias in Recruitment:** Implicit biases in hiring processes often lead to the underrepresentation of qualified candidates from diverse backgrounds.

- **Lack of Role Models:** The absence of mentors and role models in the tech industry can discourage young people from pursuing careers in technology.

## Mindful Tech Solutions' Approach

To combat these challenges, Sage Yamamoto and Mindful Tech Solutions implemented several key initiatives aimed at fostering inclusivity:

- **Scholarship Programs:** Mindful Tech established scholarship programs specifically for students from underrepresented communities. These scholarships cover tuition costs and provide access to resources such as mentorship and internships.

- **Partnerships with Educational Institutions:** Collaborating with schools and universities, Mindful Tech developed outreach programs that introduce students to technology through workshops, coding boot camps, and summer internships. These programs are designed to spark interest in tech careers and provide hands-on experience.

- **Inclusive Hiring Practices:** By implementing blind recruitment processes and training hiring managers to recognize and mitigate biases, Mindful Tech has improved the diversity of its workforce. This approach not only enhances team creativity but also ensures that a variety of perspectives are represented in decision-making processes.

- **Mentorship Programs:** Sage initiated mentorship programs that connect young professionals from underrepresented communities with experienced industry leaders. These relationships provide guidance, support, and networking opportunities that can significantly impact career trajectories.

- **Community Engagement:** Mindful Tech actively engages with local communities by sponsoring tech fairs and hackathons, providing platforms for aspiring technologists to showcase their skills and innovations. This visibility can attract interest from potential employers and investors.

## Case Study: The TechBridge Initiative

One of the hallmark projects under Sage's leadership is the TechBridge Initiative, launched in partnership with several non-profit organizations. This initiative aims to bridge the gap between education and employment for underrepresented youth in urban areas. Key components of the TechBridge Initiative include:

- **Workshops and Training:** Offering free workshops in coding, data science, and digital literacy, the initiative equips participants with the skills needed to enter the tech workforce.

- **Internship Opportunities:** Collaborating with local businesses, the initiative provides internships that allow participants to gain real-world experience and build professional networks.

- **Career Fairs:** Hosting annual career fairs that connect participants with tech companies actively seeking diverse talent. These events create pathways to employment and foster relationships between young innovators and industry leaders.

## Measuring Impact and Success

To evaluate the success of these initiatives, Mindful Tech employs a framework that includes both quantitative and qualitative metrics. Key performance indicators (KPIs) include:

- **Enrollment Rates:** Tracking the number of students from underrepresented communities enrolling in tech programs.

- **Employment Outcomes:** Monitoring job placement rates for participants in internship and mentorship programs.

- **Feedback Surveys:** Gathering qualitative data from participants to assess the effectiveness of programs and identify areas for improvement.

The results have been promising. Since the launch of the TechBridge Initiative, over 500 students have participated in workshops, with a 75% job placement rate among those who completed the program. Feedback from participants highlights increased confidence and a clearer understanding of career pathways in technology.

## Conclusion

Creating opportunities for underrepresented communities is not merely a philanthropic endeavor but a strategic imperative for the tech industry. Sage Yamamoto's commitment to fostering diversity through initiatives like the TechBridge Initiative exemplifies how ethical innovation can lead to a more inclusive and equitable tech landscape. By addressing barriers to entry and actively promoting inclusivity, Mindful Tech Solutions is paving the way for a future where the tech industry reflects the diverse society it serves.

## Ethical Leadership and Corporate Social Responsibility

In the contemporary business landscape, ethical leadership has emerged as a fundamental pillar of corporate governance, particularly within the realm of technology. Sage Yamamoto exemplifies this notion through her commitment to Corporate Social Responsibility (CSR) and ethical practices in her company, Mindful Tech Solutions. This section delves into the core principles of ethical leadership and its intersection with CSR, exploring the challenges and opportunities that arise in this domain.

### Understanding Ethical Leadership

Ethical leadership is characterized by leaders who prioritize ethical standards and values in their decision-making processes. According to Brown and Treviño (2006), ethical leaders demonstrate integrity, fairness, and a commitment to the well-being of their stakeholders. This leadership style fosters a culture of trust and accountability, encouraging employees to align their actions with the organization's ethical standards.

$$\text{Ethical Leadership} = f(\text{Integrity, Fairness, Stakeholder Well-being}) \quad (18)$$

Sage Yamamoto's approach to leadership is rooted in these principles. By promoting transparency and inclusivity within her organization, she has cultivated an environment where employees feel empowered to voice their concerns and contribute to the ethical discourse surrounding technological advancements.

## Corporate Social Responsibility: A Strategic Imperative

Corporate Social Responsibility refers to the practice of integrating social and environmental concerns into business operations and interactions with stakeholders. CSR encompasses a range of activities, from philanthropy to sustainable business practices. The World Business Council for Sustainable Development (WBCSD) defines CSR as "the continuing commitment by business to behave ethically and contribute to economic development while improving the quality of life of the workforce, their families, the local community, and society at large."

In the context of Mindful Tech Solutions, CSR initiatives include:

- **Sustainable Product Development:** Creating technology that minimizes environmental impact, such as energy-efficient devices and sustainable materials.

- **Community Engagement:** Actively participating in local initiatives and supporting educational programs focused on technology and ethics.

- **Employee Welfare:** Implementing policies that promote work-life balance, mental health resources, and equitable pay.

These initiatives not only enhance the company's reputation but also contribute to long-term profitability by fostering customer loyalty and attracting top talent.

## Challenges in Ethical Leadership and CSR

Despite the benefits of ethical leadership and CSR, organizations often face significant challenges in implementing these principles. One major obstacle is the conflict between short-term profitability and long-term ethical commitments. As businesses strive to meet quarterly financial targets, the pressure to prioritize profit over ethical considerations can lead to compromised decision-making.

$$\text{Profitability} \propto \text{Short-term Gains} - \text{Ethical Considerations} \qquad (19)$$

For instance, a tech company may opt to cut corners on data privacy to reduce costs, jeopardizing user trust and long-term sustainability. Sage Yamamoto's leadership exemplifies the balance between ethical integrity and financial success, demonstrating that it is possible to align business objectives with ethical practices.

Additionally, the lack of a universal framework for ethical decision-making poses challenges for leaders. Different stakeholders may have varying expectations regarding ethical behavior, leading to confusion and potential conflicts. To address this, Yamamoto advocates for the development of industry-wide ethical standards, fostering collaboration among tech companies to establish a shared vision for responsible innovation.

### Examples of Ethical Leadership in Practice

Sage Yamamoto's commitment to ethical leadership is evident in her initiatives at Mindful Tech Solutions. One notable example is the company's decision to prioritize user privacy in its product development process. By implementing robust data protection measures and transparent user agreements, the company has built a reputation for safeguarding user information, thus enhancing customer trust.

Another example is the establishment of the Mindful Tech Foundation, which focuses on providing resources and support for underrepresented communities in technology. This initiative not only addresses social inequalities but also creates a diverse talent pool that enriches the industry.

### Conclusion

In conclusion, ethical leadership and corporate social responsibility are integral components of Sage Yamamoto's vision for Mindful Tech Solutions. By prioritizing ethical practices, fostering a culture of accountability, and engaging in meaningful CSR initiatives, she demonstrates that technology can be harnessed for positive societal impact. As the tech industry continues to evolve, the principles of ethical leadership and CSR will play a crucial role in shaping a sustainable and equitable future.

# Sharing Wisdom and Inspiring Others

## Speaking Engagements and Thought Leadership

Sage Yamamoto has established herself as a prominent voice in the realm of ethical technology through a series of impactful speaking engagements and thought leadership initiatives. With the rapid evolution of technology, the discourse surrounding its ethical implications has become increasingly critical. Yamamoto's contributions have provided clarity, inspiration, and a roadmap for navigating the complex landscape of mindful tech.

## The Role of Public Speaking in Advocacy

Public speaking serves as a powerful tool for advocacy, allowing innovators like Yamamoto to communicate their vision and influence a broad audience. In her talks, she often emphasizes the necessity of integrating ethics into technological development. According to the *Technology Acceptance Model* (TAM), perceived usefulness and perceived ease of use are fundamental factors influencing technology adoption [?]. Yamamoto expands this model by incorporating ethical considerations, positing that the perceived ethical implications of technology can significantly affect user acceptance and trust.

## Key Themes in Yamamoto's Talks

Yamamoto's speeches often revolve around several key themes:

- **The Ethical Responsibility of Innovators:** She argues that technology creators must acknowledge their role in shaping societal values. This responsibility extends beyond product development to include considerations of social impact, privacy, and user well-being.

- **Mindfulness in Tech Design:** Drawing from mindfulness practices, Yamamoto encourages technologists to design with empathy. By understanding user experiences and potential consequences, innovators can create technologies that enhance, rather than detract from, human life.

- **Collaboration Across Disciplines:** Yamamoto advocates for interdisciplinary collaboration, bringing together technologists, ethicists, social scientists, and the public to co-create solutions that are ethically sound and socially beneficial.

## Examples of Speaking Engagements

Yamamoto has been featured at numerous high-profile conferences and panels, including:

- **The Global Tech Ethics Summit:** Here, she presented her framework for ethical innovation, which combines technological advancement with a commitment to social responsibility. Her talk, titled "Innovating with Integrity," emphasized the need for ethical guidelines in AI development.

- **The Mindful Technology Conference:** Yamamoto led a workshop on "Designing for Humanity," where participants explored techniques for incorporating mindfulness into tech design processes. The workshop included hands-on activities that encouraged participants to envision user-centered products.
- **TEDx Talks:** In her TEDx talk, "The Future of Tech is Mindful," she outlined the potential societal impacts of neglecting ethical considerations in tech. She presented case studies illustrating both the benefits and pitfalls of technology, urging the audience to consider the long-term implications of their innovations.

## Influence on Policy and Industry Standards

Through her speaking engagements, Yamamoto has influenced both policy and industry standards. She has collaborated with organizations to draft ethical guidelines for technology development, emphasizing the importance of transparency and accountability. For instance, her advocacy played a pivotal role in the creation of the *Ethical AI Framework*, which provides a set of principles for responsible AI deployment [?].

## Mentorship and Educational Outreach

In addition to public speaking, Yamamoto is committed to mentorship and educational outreach. She regularly engages with universities and educational institutions, delivering guest lectures and participating in panel discussions. Her efforts aim to inspire the next generation of innovators to prioritize ethics in their work.

$$\text{Ethical Innovation} = \text{Technological Advancement} + \text{Social Responsibility} \quad (20)$$

This equation encapsulates Yamamoto's philosophy: that true innovation must harmonize technological progress with ethical considerations. By instilling these values in students and young professionals, she is cultivating a new wave of mindful tech leaders.

## Conclusion

Sage Yamamoto's speaking engagements and thought leadership have significantly shaped the conversation around ethical technology. By advocating for mindfulness in tech design and emphasizing the ethical responsibilities of innovators, she is not only influencing current practices but also inspiring a future generation committed to creating technology that serves humanity. Her work exemplifies how thought leadership can drive meaningful change in the tech industry, paving the way for a more ethical and mindful future.

## Publishing Books on Tech Ethics and Mindfulness

In the realm of technology, where rapid advancements often outpace ethical considerations, Sage Yamamoto recognized the critical need for discourse on tech ethics and mindfulness. Through his publications, he aimed to bridge the gap between innovation and responsibility, providing a roadmap for future innovators.

## Theoretical Foundations

Yamamoto's works are grounded in several key theoretical frameworks. One such framework is the **Ethics of Care**, which emphasizes the importance of interpersonal relationships and the moral significance of care in technology design. This theory posits that technology should not only serve functional purposes but also consider the well-being of users and communities.

Another foundational theory in Yamamoto's writing is **Utilitarianism**, which advocates for actions that maximize overall happiness. In the context of technology, this translates to creating products that enhance user experience while minimizing harm. Yamamoto often cites the equation:

$$U = \sum_{i=1}^{n} \frac{H_i}{C_i}$$

where $U$ represents the overall utility of a technology, $H_i$ denotes the happiness generated for each user $i$, and $C_i$ signifies the costs associated with that happiness. This equation encapsulates the delicate balance between benefits and drawbacks inherent in tech development.

## Addressing Problems in Tech Ethics

Yamamoto's publications tackle pressing issues in the tech industry, such as data privacy, algorithmic bias, and the environmental impact of technological waste. For instance, in his book *Ethical Algorithms: Navigating Bias in Machine Learning*, he discusses the pervasive issue of bias in AI systems. He emphasizes that algorithms, often perceived as objective, can perpetuate existing societal inequalities if not designed with ethical considerations in mind.

He presents a case study on a widely-used facial recognition software that misidentifies individuals from marginalized communities at disproportionately higher rates. This example serves as a poignant reminder of the ethical implications of neglecting diversity in data sets and highlights the necessity of inclusive design practices.

## Mindfulness in Tech Design

In his work *Mindful Tech: Designing for Well-Being*, Yamamoto advocates for integrating mindfulness into the design process. He argues that technology should foster a sense of presence and well-being rather than distraction and anxiety. He introduces the concept of **Digital Mindfulness**, which encourages users to engage with technology in a way that enhances their quality of life.

Yamamoto outlines practical strategies for implementing mindfulness in tech design, such as:

- **User-Centric Design:** Involving users in the design process to ensure their needs and values are prioritized.

- **Feedback Loops:** Creating systems that allow users to provide feedback on their experiences, enabling continuous improvement.

- **Mindful Notifications:** Designing notifications that are respectful of users' time and attention, minimizing disruptions.

## Examples of Impactful Publications

Yamamoto's influence extends beyond theoretical discussions. His books have inspired a generation of tech innovators to adopt ethical practices. For example, in *The Responsible Innovator: Ethics in the Age of AI*, he profiles several startups that have successfully integrated ethical considerations into their business models.

One notable example is a company that developed an app to promote mental health awareness. By leveraging user data responsibly and prioritizing user privacy, the app not only provided valuable resources but also fostered a supportive community. This case exemplifies how ethical innovation can lead to both business success and positive societal impact.

## Conclusion

Through his publications, Sage Yamamoto has made significant contributions to the discourse on tech ethics and mindfulness. By addressing critical issues and providing actionable insights, he has empowered future innovators to prioritize ethical considerations in their work. His call for a more mindful approach to technology resonates deeply in an era where the consequences of neglecting ethics can be profound. As Yamamoto continues to write and inspire, his legacy as a thought leader in tech ethics will undoubtedly shape the future of the industry.

## Becoming a Mentor to the Next Generation of Innovators

In the rapidly evolving landscape of technology, mentorship plays a crucial role in shaping the future of innovation. Sage Yamamoto recognized early on that sharing knowledge and experience with budding innovators is essential for fostering a culture of ethical and mindful technology. This section explores the significance of mentorship in the tech industry, the challenges faced by both mentors and mentees, and the ways in which Sage has actively contributed to nurturing the next generation of ethical thinkers.

### The Importance of Mentorship

Mentorship serves as a bridge between experience and innovation. According to a study by Allen et al. (2004), individuals who receive mentorship are more likely to experience career advancement, increased job satisfaction, and enhanced professional networks. In the context of technology, where rapid advancements can lead to ethical dilemmas, the guidance of seasoned innovators like Sage is invaluable. Mentorship not only imparts technical skills but also instills a sense of ethical responsibility in the next generation.

### Challenges in Mentorship

Despite its benefits, mentorship in the tech industry is fraught with challenges. One significant issue is the diversity gap in tech, where underrepresented groups often lack access to mentorship opportunities. A report by the Kapor Center for Social Impact (2017) highlights that only 10% of tech workers are Black or Latinx, underscoring the need for mentors who can provide support and guidance to these communities.

Another challenge is the fast-paced nature of technological advancements. Mentors must stay updated with the latest trends and ethical considerations to provide relevant advice. This can be particularly taxing for established professionals who are already balancing their responsibilities in a demanding industry.

## Sage's Approach to Mentorship

Sage Yamamoto has adopted a proactive approach to mentorship, focusing on inclusivity and accessibility. By partnering with educational institutions and community organizations, Sage has created programs that connect aspiring innovators with experienced professionals. One notable initiative is the "Mindful Tech Mentorship Program," which pairs students from underrepresented backgrounds with industry leaders.

Through this program, Sage emphasizes the importance of ethical considerations in technology. Mentees are encouraged to explore questions such as:

$$\text{How can technology enhance human well-being?} \tag{21}$$

$$\text{What ethical dilemmas arise from emerging technologies?} \tag{22}$$

These questions guide discussions and projects, allowing mentees to engage critically with the implications of their work.

## Case Study: The Impact of Mentorship

A compelling example of Sage's mentorship can be seen in the story of Maya Chen, a young innovator who developed a mindfulness app aimed at reducing anxiety among teens. Under Sage's guidance, Maya navigated the complexities of app development while considering the ethical implications of data privacy and user consent.

Maya's project not only gained traction but also sparked conversations about the importance of mental health in the tech industry. Sage's mentorship helped her understand that innovation should be driven by a desire to improve lives, not merely by profit motives.

## Fostering a Culture of Ethical Innovation

Sage's mentorship extends beyond individual relationships. By advocating for a culture of ethical innovation within organizations, Sage encourages mentees to take ownership of their work and its impact on society. This involves:

- Encouraging open discussions about ethical dilemmas in technology.

- Providing resources for understanding the societal implications of tech innovations.

- Promoting collaboration among diverse teams to foster innovative solutions.

Through these efforts, Sage aims to cultivate a new generation of innovators who prioritize ethical considerations in their work.

## Conclusion

In conclusion, becoming a mentor to the next generation of innovators is a vital component of Sage Yamamoto's legacy. By addressing the challenges of mentorship and actively engaging with aspiring technologists, Sage not only imparts knowledge but also inspires a commitment to ethical practices in technology. As the industry continues to evolve, the role of mentorship will be crucial in shaping a future where innovation aligns with the greater good, ensuring that technology serves humanity rather than the other way around.

## Collaborating with Educational Institutions

Sage Yamamoto recognized early on that the future of ethical innovation in technology would heavily rely on the education and preparation of the next generation of innovators. Collaborating with educational institutions became a cornerstone of his mission to spread the principles of mindful tech and ethical practices. This collaboration took various forms, including partnerships with universities, workshops, and the development of curricula aimed at integrating ethics into technology education.

## Theoretical Foundations

The theoretical basis for these collaborations can be drawn from several frameworks, including Constructivist Learning Theory, which posits that learners construct knowledge through experiences and reflections. Vygotsky's Social Development Theory also plays a crucial role, emphasizing the importance of social interaction and cultural context in learning. By engaging with students in collaborative projects, Sage aimed to create a learning environment where students could explore the ethical dimensions of technology through real-world applications.

## Challenges in Collaboration

Despite the potential benefits, collaborating with educational institutions posed several challenges. One significant issue was the gap between academic theory and practical application. Many educational programs focus on technical skills, often neglecting the ethical implications of technology. This disconnect can lead to graduates who are technically proficient but lack the critical thinking skills necessary to navigate ethical dilemmas in their future careers.

Another challenge was resistance from educational institutions to change their established curricula. Many universities have rigid structures that make it difficult to incorporate new subjects or methodologies, particularly those that challenge traditional views of technology as purely a tool for efficiency and profit.

## Examples of Successful Collaborations

To address these challenges, Sage initiated several successful collaborations with educational institutions. One notable example was the partnership with the University of California, Berkeley, where he helped develop a course titled "Ethics in Technology: Mindful Innovation." This course combined theoretical discussions with hands-on projects, allowing students to work on real-world problems while considering the ethical implications of their solutions. The curriculum included case studies on data privacy, algorithmic bias, and the societal impacts of emerging technologies.

Additionally, Sage collaborated with high schools to introduce a program called "Tech for Good." This initiative aimed to inspire younger students to think critically about technology's role in society. The program included workshops where students designed apps that addressed social issues, such as mental health awareness and environmental sustainability. By engaging students in meaningful projects, Sage hoped to instill a sense of responsibility and encourage them to consider the broader implications of their work.

## Long-term Impact

The long-term impact of these collaborations is evident in the growing number of educational institutions that have begun to prioritize ethics in their technology programs. As a result of Sage's efforts, several universities have established dedicated centers for ethical technology research and education. These centers not only conduct research on the implications of technology but also serve as incubators for startups focused on ethical innovation.

Furthermore, the partnerships have fostered a culture of interdisciplinary collaboration, where students from different fields—such as computer science, philosophy, and social sciences—come together to tackle complex problems. This approach aligns with the idea of "T-shaped" professionals, who possess deep knowledge in one area while also having a broad understanding of other disciplines, enabling them to approach challenges holistically.

## Conclusion

In conclusion, Sage Yamamoto's collaborations with educational institutions exemplify a proactive approach to shaping the future of technology through ethical education. By addressing the challenges of integrating ethics into technology curricula and providing practical experiences for students, these partnerships have laid the groundwork for a generation of innovators who are not only skilled in technology but also committed to making ethical decisions. This commitment is essential for fostering a more mindful and responsible tech landscape, where innovation serves humanity rather than undermining it.

## Advocating for Ethical Standards in the Tech Industry

In an era where technology permeates every aspect of our lives, the call for ethical standards in the tech industry has never been more pressing. Sage Yamamoto, through her various initiatives, has championed the need for ethical frameworks that guide technological development, ensuring that innovation does not come at the expense of societal values or individual rights.

### The Necessity of Ethical Standards

The rapid advancement of technology has outpaced the establishment of regulatory frameworks, leading to numerous ethical dilemmas. Issues such as data privacy, algorithmic bias, and the exploitation of user information have emerged as significant concerns. For instance, the Cambridge Analytica scandal highlighted the potential for misuse of personal data, raising questions about consent and transparency in data handling. As pointed out by [?], this situation exemplifies the "surveillance capitalism" that has emerged, where personal data becomes a commodity exploited for profit.

The necessity of ethical standards can be understood through the lens of *Utilitarianism*, which advocates for actions that maximize overall happiness. In the tech context, this means creating products that not only serve business interests but also promote user welfare. A failure to do so can lead to societal harm, as seen in the case of social media platforms contributing to mental health issues among users, particularly adolescents.

## Key Challenges in Establishing Standards

Despite the clear need for ethical standards, several challenges hinder their implementation:

- **Diverse Stakeholder Interests:** The tech industry comprises various stakeholders, including corporations, consumers, and governments, each with differing priorities. For example, while consumers may prioritize privacy, companies often focus on profitability, leading to conflicts in ethical considerations.

- **Rapid Technological Change:** The pace of innovation often leaves little time for ethical considerations to catch up. Technologies like artificial intelligence (AI) and machine learning evolve quickly, complicating the establishment of static ethical guidelines.

- **Global Disparities:** Different countries have varying cultural values and legal frameworks, making it challenging to create universal ethical standards. For instance, data protection laws in the European Union, such as the General Data Protection Regulation (GDPR), differ significantly from those in the United States, where data privacy is less regulated.

## Sage Yamamoto's Advocacy Efforts

Sage Yamamoto has taken a proactive stance in advocating for ethical standards within the tech industry. Her approach includes:

- **Collaborative Frameworks:** Yamamoto promotes the development of collaborative frameworks that involve stakeholders from different sectors. By fostering dialogue between tech companies, policymakers, and civil society, she aims to create comprehensive ethical guidelines that reflect diverse perspectives.

- **Education and Training:** Recognizing that ethical considerations must be ingrained in the tech workforce, Yamamoto has initiated programs aimed at educating developers and engineers about the ethical implications of their work. This includes integrating ethics into computer science curricula and providing workshops on responsible innovation.

- **Public Awareness Campaigns:** Yamamoto has launched campaigns to raise public awareness about the importance of ethical standards in technology. By informing consumers about their rights and the ethical implications of their digital interactions, she empowers them to demand better practices from tech companies.

## The Role of Policy and Regulation

While individual advocacy is crucial, the role of policy and regulation cannot be overlooked. Governments must enact laws that enforce ethical standards across the tech industry. For instance, the *Ethics Guidelines for Trustworthy AI* published by the European Commission outlines key requirements for AI systems, including transparency, accountability, and fairness. Such regulatory frameworks can provide a baseline for ethical practices, ensuring that companies prioritize societal well-being alongside profitability.

Furthermore, the establishment of independent ethical review boards, similar to those in medical research, could help assess the ethical implications of new technologies before they are deployed. This proactive approach could mitigate potential harm and foster a culture of responsibility within the tech industry.

## Conclusion

Advocating for ethical standards in the tech industry is not merely a moral obligation; it is essential for the sustainability of technological innovation. As Sage Yamamoto continues to lead by example, her efforts serve as a blueprint for integrating ethical considerations into the fabric of technology development. The journey towards a more ethical tech landscape requires collective action from all stakeholders, emphasizing that technology should ultimately serve humanity, not the other way around. By prioritizing ethical standards, the tech industry can foster trust, enhance user well-being, and contribute positively to society.

# Chapter Five: Legacy and Future

## Building a Lasting Legacy

### Establishing the Sage Yamamoto Foundation

The establishment of the Sage Yamamoto Foundation marked a pivotal moment in the journey of ethical innovation, serving as a beacon of hope and a catalyst for change in the tech industry. Founded in 2040, the foundation was created with the explicit mission to promote ethical practices in technology, support sustainable innovations, and foster a culture of responsibility among tech entrepreneurs.

### Mission and Vision

The foundation's mission is rooted in the belief that technology should enhance human well-being and contribute positively to society. The vision is to create a world where ethical considerations are at the forefront of technological advancements. The foundation aims to bridge the gap between innovation and ethics, ensuring that future technologies are developed with mindfulness and responsibility.

### Core Programs

To achieve its mission, the Sage Yamamoto Foundation developed several core programs:

- **Ethical Tech Incubator:** This program provides resources, mentorship, and funding to startups that prioritize ethical considerations in their technology development. By fostering a supportive environment, the incubator aims to nurture the next generation of ethical innovators.

- **Sustainable Technology Grants:** The foundation allocates grants to projects that focus on sustainability and environmental responsibility. These grants encourage innovators to develop technologies that not only meet market demands but also contribute to ecological preservation.

- **Education and Outreach:** Through workshops, seminars, and online courses, the foundation educates entrepreneurs, students, and the general public about the importance of ethical innovation. This outreach program emphasizes the need for a collective approach to ethical standards in technology.

- **Research and Advocacy:** The foundation supports research initiatives that explore the ethical implications of emerging technologies. By collaborating with academic institutions, the foundation advocates for policies that promote ethical practices within the tech industry.

## Impact on the Tech Community

The establishment of the Sage Yamamoto Foundation has had a profound impact on the tech community. By fostering a culture of ethical responsibility, the foundation has inspired numerous startups to integrate ethical considerations into their business models. For example, a tech startup focused on AI ethics received funding through the Ethical Tech Incubator and subsequently developed a groundbreaking AI framework that prioritizes user privacy and data security.

## Challenges and Solutions

Despite its successes, the foundation faced challenges in promoting ethical innovation. One significant problem was the pervasive mindset within the tech industry that prioritizes profit over ethics. To combat this, the foundation implemented a multi-faceted approach:

- **Partnerships with Industry Leaders:** By collaborating with established tech companies, the foundation aimed to influence industry standards and practices. These partnerships facilitated the sharing of resources and knowledge, creating a ripple effect of ethical awareness.

- **Public Campaigns:** The foundation launched public awareness campaigns highlighting the importance of ethical practices in technology. These campaigns utilized social media, podcasts, and public speaking engagements to reach a broad audience, emphasizing the long-term benefits of ethical innovation.

- **Policy Advocacy:** Engaging with policymakers, the foundation advocated for regulations that support ethical practices in the tech industry. This included lobbying for data protection laws and transparency requirements for tech companies.

## Case Studies

Several case studies illustrate the foundation's impact:

1. **Project EcoTech:** A startup that received a Sustainable Technology Grant developed an eco-friendly data center that uses renewable energy sources. This project not only reduced carbon emissions but also set a new standard for sustainability in the tech industry.

2. **Mindful AI Initiative:** A tech firm, supported by the Ethical Tech Incubator, launched an AI-driven mental health application designed to provide users with personalized mindfulness exercises. The app incorporates ethical guidelines to ensure user data privacy and mental well-being.

3. **Tech for Good Conference:** The foundation organized an annual conference that brings together innovators, policymakers, and thought leaders to discuss the future of ethical technology. The conference has grown significantly, attracting thousands of participants and fostering collaborations across sectors.

## Future Directions

Looking ahead, the Sage Yamamoto Foundation aims to expand its reach and influence. Plans include:

- **Global Expansion:** Establishing partnerships with international organizations to promote ethical tech practices worldwide. This global perspective will enhance the foundation's impact and foster a diverse network of ethical innovators.

- **Enhanced Research Initiatives:** Increasing funding for research on the societal impacts of emerging technologies, particularly in areas like artificial intelligence, biotechnology, and data privacy.

- **Collaboration with Educational Institutions:** Strengthening ties with universities to develop curricula focused on ethical technology, ensuring that future generations of tech leaders are equipped with the necessary tools to navigate ethical dilemmas.

The establishment of the Sage Yamamoto Foundation signifies a commitment to a more ethical and mindful future in technology. By championing ethical innovation, the foundation not only honors Sage Yamamoto's legacy but also paves the way for a new era of responsible technology that prioritizes humanity's well-being.

## Fostering Ethical Tech Startups

In the contemporary landscape of technology, the emergence of ethical tech startups represents a paradigm shift towards innovation that prioritizes societal well-being alongside profit. Sage Yamamoto, through her visionary leadership, has played a pivotal role in fostering such startups, creating an ecosystem where ethical considerations are at the forefront of technological development.

### The Importance of Ethical Startups

Ethical tech startups are crucial for addressing the myriad challenges that arise from rapid technological advancement. These challenges include issues such as data privacy, algorithmic bias, and the environmental impact of technology. By embedding ethical principles into their core business models, these startups can mitigate risks and promote a more sustainable and equitable technological future.

A seminal theory in this domain is the *Triple Bottom Line* (TBL) framework, which posits that businesses should focus on three bottom lines: profit, people, and planet. This holistic approach encourages startups to evaluate their impact not just in terms of financial success, but also in relation to social and environmental outcomes. The equation for the TBL can be expressed as:

$$TBL = \text{Profit} + \text{People} + \text{Planet} \qquad (23)$$

This framework has been instrumental in guiding ethical tech startups to measure their success through a broader lens.

### Challenges Faced by Ethical Startups

Despite the noble intentions behind ethical tech startups, they encounter numerous challenges that can hinder their growth. One significant problem is the difficulty in securing funding. Traditional investors often prioritize high returns, which can lead to a reluctance to invest in ventures that emphasize ethical practices over rapid profitability. This creates a funding gap for startups committed to ethical innovation.

Moreover, ethical startups frequently face the challenge of navigating a competitive landscape dominated by larger, established companies that may not prioritize ethical considerations. These giants can leverage their resources to outcompete smaller startups, making it difficult for them to gain market share.

## Strategies for Fostering Ethical Startups

To overcome these challenges, several strategies can be employed:

1. **Building a Supportive Ecosystem:** Creating networks of ethical investors, mentors, and incubators can provide startups with the resources and guidance needed to thrive. For instance, organizations like *The Impact Hub* and *Techstars* have begun focusing on ethical startups, offering funding and mentorship tailored to their unique needs.

2. **Promoting Transparency and Accountability:** Ethical startups should prioritize transparency in their operations and decision-making processes. By implementing frameworks for accountability, such as third-party audits and impact assessments, these startups can build trust with consumers and investors alike.

3. **Leveraging Technology for Social Good:** Ethical tech startups can harness emerging technologies, such as blockchain and artificial intelligence, to address social issues. For example, *Everledger* utilizes blockchain to create a transparent supply chain for diamonds, ensuring ethical sourcing and reducing fraud.

4. **Advocating for Policy Changes:** Engaging in advocacy for regulations that support ethical practices in technology can create a more favorable environment for ethical startups. Collaborating with policymakers to establish standards for data privacy and ethical AI can level the playing field.

## Case Studies of Successful Ethical Startups

Several ethical tech startups exemplify the principles and strategies outlined above.

- **Patagonia:** While primarily an outdoor apparel company, Patagonia has ventured into technology with initiatives focused on environmental sustainability. Their *Worn Wear* program encourages the repair and reuse of clothing, reducing waste and promoting a circular economy.

- **Tala:** This fintech startup provides microloans to underserved populations in emerging markets, leveraging technology to promote financial inclusion. Tala's model emphasizes ethical lending practices and transparency, helping to empower individuals economically.

- **Olio:** A food-sharing app that connects neighbors to share surplus food, Olio addresses food waste while fostering community engagement. By using technology to facilitate sharing, Olio exemplifies how startups can create social value alongside business success.

## Conclusion

Fostering ethical tech startups is essential for creating a future where technology serves humanity rather than undermines it. Through strategic support, advocacy, and the application of ethical frameworks, innovators like Sage Yamamoto are leading the charge toward a more responsible and sustainable tech landscape. By prioritizing ethical considerations, these startups not only contribute to societal well-being but also pave the way for a new era of innovation that aligns with the values of a conscientious society.

## Advancing the Field of Ethical Innovation

In the rapidly evolving landscape of technology, the necessity for ethical innovation has become increasingly apparent. Sage Yamamoto's commitment to advancing this field stems from a profound understanding of the intersection between technological progress and ethical responsibility. This section delves into the frameworks, theories, and practical examples that illustrate how ethical innovation can be effectively integrated into the tech industry.

### Theoretical Frameworks

At the core of ethical innovation lies a variety of philosophical theories that guide decision-making processes. One prominent framework is Utilitarianism, which posits that the best action is the one that maximizes overall happiness or well-being. In the context of technology, this means designing products and services that enhance user experience while minimizing harm. For instance, when developing social media platforms, companies can apply utilitarian principles by prioritizing features that promote mental health and well-being over addictive engagement metrics.

Another critical framework is Deontological ethics, particularly the work of Immanuel Kant, which emphasizes the importance of duty and moral rules. This approach advocates for the intrinsic value of individuals, suggesting that technology should respect user autonomy and privacy. For example, ethical data handling practices must be established, ensuring that users are informed and consent to how their data is used. This is particularly relevant in the age of big data, where companies often prioritize profit over ethical considerations.

## Identifying Problems in Ethical Innovation

Despite the theoretical frameworks available, numerous challenges hinder the advancement of ethical innovation. One significant problem is the "innovation trap," where companies prioritize rapid technological advancement at the expense of ethical considerations. This often leads to products that may be harmful or exploitative. For instance, facial recognition technology has raised concerns about privacy violations and racial bias, prompting calls for stricter regulations and ethical guidelines.

Moreover, there exists a pervasive lack of diversity within tech companies, which can lead to blind spots in ethical considerations. Research has shown that diverse teams are more likely to identify potential ethical issues and create inclusive products. For example, the lack of representation in AI development has resulted in biased algorithms that disproportionately affect marginalized communities. Addressing this issue requires a commitment to fostering diverse teams and inclusive practices in the innovation process.

## Examples of Ethical Innovation in Practice

Sage Yamamoto has championed several initiatives that exemplify ethical innovation. One notable example is the development of a social media platform focused on mental well-being. Unlike traditional platforms that often prioritize engagement at any cost, this platform integrates features that promote positive interactions and mindfulness. Users are encouraged to take breaks, engage in meaningful conversations, and access resources for mental health support. The success of this platform demonstrates that ethical considerations can lead to sustainable business models and user loyalty.

Another example is the implementation of ethical AI in healthcare. By leveraging AI technology to assist in diagnosing diseases, ethical considerations were paramount in ensuring that the algorithms used were free from bias and respected patient privacy. Collaborating with healthcare professionals and ethicists, Sage's team developed a system that not only improved diagnostic accuracy but also maintained the highest standards of patient confidentiality.

## Policy Advocacy and Ethical Standards

Advancing the field of ethical innovation also requires active engagement in policy advocacy. Sage Yamamoto has been a vocal proponent of establishing industry-wide ethical standards that govern technology development. This includes advocating for regulations that ensure transparency in AI decision-making processes and the ethical use of data. By collaborating with policymakers, industry leaders, and academic institutions, Yamamoto has worked to create a framework that encourages responsible innovation.

Furthermore, fostering a culture of ethical responsibility within organizations is crucial. This involves creating internal policies that prioritize ethical considerations in product development and decision-making processes. Companies can implement ethics training programs that educate employees about the importance of ethical innovation and empower them to voice concerns regarding potential ethical dilemmas.

## Conclusion

In conclusion, advancing the field of ethical innovation is a multifaceted endeavor that requires a combination of theoretical frameworks, practical applications, and policy advocacy. Sage Yamamoto's contributions have paved the way for a more mindful approach to technology, emphasizing the importance of ethical considerations in every stage of innovation. As the tech industry continues to evolve, the commitment to ethical innovation will not only enhance societal well-being but also ensure a sustainable and responsible future for technology.

## Engaging in Policy Advocacy for Tech Ethics

In the rapidly evolving landscape of technology, the need for ethical guidelines and regulations has never been more pressing. Sage Yamamoto recognized early on that engaging in policy advocacy for tech ethics was a vital component of her mission. As technological advancements continue to outpace legislative frameworks, the gap between innovation and regulation creates significant ethical dilemmas that require immediate attention.

## The Importance of Policy Advocacy

Policy advocacy serves as a bridge between technological innovation and societal values. By actively participating in the policy-making process, innovators like Sage can ensure that ethical considerations are integrated into the development and deployment of new technologies. This approach not only protects consumers but also fosters a culture of responsibility within the tech industry.

One of the primary theories underpinning the need for policy advocacy in tech ethics is the **Stakeholder Theory**. This theory posits that organizations should consider the interests of all stakeholders, including users, employees, and the broader community, rather than focusing solely on profit maximization. Engaging in policy advocacy allows innovators to represent these diverse interests and promote ethical standards that benefit society as a whole.

## Addressing Key Problems

Several pressing issues highlight the necessity of policy advocacy in tech ethics:

- **Data Privacy:** With the rise of big data and surveillance technologies, concerns about user privacy have escalated. Innovators must advocate for policies that protect personal data and ensure transparency in data collection practices. For instance, the General Data Protection Regulation (GDPR) in the European Union serves as a benchmark for data protection, but its global implementation remains inconsistent.

- **Algorithmic Bias:** As algorithms increasingly dictate outcomes in areas such as hiring, lending, and law enforcement, the potential for bias and discrimination becomes a critical concern. Advocating for policies that require algorithmic accountability and fairness can help mitigate these risks. An example is the Algorithmic Accountability Act proposed in the United States, which seeks to mandate audits of automated decision-making systems.

- **Digital Divide:** The rapid advancement of technology has exacerbated inequalities in access to digital resources. Policy advocacy can play a crucial role in promoting equitable access to technology, particularly for underserved communities. Initiatives such as the Federal Communications Commission's (FCC) Lifeline program aim to provide affordable internet access to low-income households.

## Strategies for Effective Advocacy

To effectively engage in policy advocacy for tech ethics, innovators like Sage Yamamoto employ several strategies:

1. **Building Coalitions:** Collaborating with other ethical innovators, non-profit organizations, and academic institutions can amplify advocacy efforts. By forming coalitions, stakeholders can present a united front to policymakers, making it more challenging to ignore ethical concerns.

2. **Research and Evidence-Based Advocacy:** Providing data-driven insights into the impact of technology on society strengthens advocacy efforts. By conducting research that highlights the ethical implications of specific technologies, innovators can inform policymakers and encourage the development of sound regulations.

3. **Public Engagement:** Raising public awareness about ethical issues in technology fosters a culture of accountability. Through speaking engagements, social media campaigns, and community outreach, innovators can mobilize public support for ethical policies and practices.

4. **Direct Lobbying:** Engaging directly with legislators and regulatory bodies is essential for influencing policy decisions. Innovators can provide expert testimony, participate in public hearings, and submit policy recommendations to ensure that ethical considerations are prioritized in legislative processes.

## Examples of Successful Advocacy

Sage Yamamoto's advocacy efforts have led to several notable achievements in the realm of tech ethics:

- **The Ethical Tech Coalition:** By founding this coalition, Sage brought together diverse stakeholders to advocate for ethical standards in technology. The coalition successfully lobbied for the introduction of an ethical review board within tech companies to assess the implications of new products before their launch.

- **The Tech Ethics Summit:** Organizing an annual summit that gathers policymakers, technologists, and ethicists has facilitated meaningful dialogue around pressing ethical issues. The summit has resulted in actionable policy proposals that have been adopted at both local and national levels.

- **Educational Initiatives:** Sage has partnered with educational institutions to develop curricula focused on tech ethics, ensuring that the next generation of innovators is equipped with the knowledge and skills needed to navigate ethical dilemmas in technology.

## Conclusion

Engaging in policy advocacy for tech ethics is not just an option; it is a responsibility that innovators must embrace. By addressing critical issues such as data privacy, algorithmic bias, and the digital divide, and by employing effective advocacy strategies, innovators like Sage Yamamoto can shape a future where technology serves the greater good. As the tech landscape continues to evolve, the importance of ethical advocacy will only grow, demanding a proactive and collaborative approach to ensure that innovation aligns with societal values.

## Inspiring a Culture of Ethical Responsibility

In the rapidly evolving landscape of technology, fostering a culture of ethical responsibility has become paramount. Sage Yamamoto, through her initiatives and leadership, has set a precedent for how tech companies can integrate ethical considerations into their core operations. This section explores the principles and practices that Sage employed to inspire a culture of ethical responsibility, the challenges faced in this endeavor, and the broader implications for the tech industry.

### Principles of Ethical Responsibility

At the heart of Sage's philosophy is the belief that ethical responsibility is not merely an add-on but an integral part of the innovation process. This is encapsulated in the following principles:

- **Transparency:** Open communication about company practices and decision-making processes fosters trust among stakeholders. Sage implemented regular town hall meetings to discuss ethical dilemmas and the company's stance on various issues.

- **Accountability:** Establishing clear lines of responsibility ensures that individuals within the organization are held accountable for their actions. Sage introduced an internal ethics committee that reviews projects for ethical implications before they are launched.

- **Inclusivity:** Encouraging diverse perspectives in decision-making processes can lead to more ethical outcomes. Sage actively sought input from employees at all levels and from various backgrounds, ensuring that multiple viewpoints were considered.

- **Continuous Learning:** The tech industry is constantly changing; therefore, ongoing education about ethical practices is crucial. Sage partnered with educational institutions to provide workshops and training on ethical technology use and development.

## Challenges in Cultivating Ethical Responsibility

Despite the clear benefits of fostering an ethical culture, Sage faced several challenges:

- **Resistance to Change:** Many employees were accustomed to traditional business practices that prioritized profit over ethics. To combat this, Sage initiated a series of workshops that highlighted the long-term benefits of ethical practices, including case studies of companies that suffered due to ethical lapses.

- **Balancing Profit and Ethics:** In a competitive industry, the pressure to prioritize profit can undermine ethical initiatives. Sage addressed this by developing a framework for evaluating projects that weighed ethical considerations alongside financial projections. This framework is mathematically represented as:

$$E = \frac{P + I}{C} \qquad (24)$$

where $E$ is the ethical score, $P$ is the profit potential, $I$ is the potential impact on society, and $C$ is the cost of ethical implementation. Projects that achieved a high ethical score were prioritized.

- **External Pressures:** The tech industry is often influenced by market demands that may not align with ethical considerations. Sage advocated for a shift in consumer expectations by launching campaigns that highlighted the importance of ethical tech, thereby creating a demand for responsible innovation.

## Examples of Ethical Responsibility in Action

Sage Yamamoto's commitment to ethical responsibility yielded tangible results. One notable example was the redesign of a popular social media platform to promote mental well-being. By incorporating features that encouraged users to take breaks and engage in mindfulness practices, the platform not only enhanced user experience but also demonstrated that ethical considerations can lead to innovative solutions.

Another example is the development of a healthcare application that prioritized patient privacy and data security. Sage's team adopted a user-centric approach, ensuring that patients had control over their data and were informed about how their information would be used. This initiative not only built trust with users but also set a new standard for privacy in healthcare technology.

## Broader Implications for the Tech Industry

Sage's efforts to inspire a culture of ethical responsibility extend beyond her company. By collaborating with other innovators and sharing her framework for ethical decision-making, she has contributed to a growing movement within the tech industry. This movement emphasizes that ethical innovation can coexist with profitability, ultimately leading to sustainable business practices that benefit society as a whole.

The impact of these initiatives is reflected in the increasing number of tech companies adopting similar ethical frameworks. As the industry evolves, the expectation for ethical responsibility will likely become a standard practice rather than an exception.

## Conclusion

Inspiring a culture of ethical responsibility is not a one-time effort but an ongoing commitment that requires dedication, transparency, and collaboration. Through her leadership, Sage Yamamoto has demonstrated that it is possible to integrate ethics into the very fabric of technological innovation. As the tech industry continues to face ethical dilemmas, her legacy serves as a guiding light for future innovators, reminding them that the pursuit of profit should never come at the expense of ethical integrity. The call to action is clear: the future of technology must be built on a foundation of ethical responsibility, ensuring that innovation serves humanity rather than undermines it.

## Looking Ahead

### Predicting the Future Impacts of Mindful Tech

As we look toward the future, the implications of mindful technology—an approach that prioritizes ethical considerations in the development and deployment of technology—are poised to be profound and far-reaching. The trajectory of technological innovation has historically been marked by rapid advancements that often outpace societal understanding and regulatory frameworks. However, the emergence of mindful tech represents a paradigm shift, one that seeks to harmonize technological progress with human values and ethical standards.

### Theoretical Foundations

The theoretical underpinning of mindful tech can be traced to various fields, including ethics, psychology, and systems theory. One of the central theories is the *Technological Determinism* theory, which posits that technology shapes society in significant ways. However, mindful tech introduces a counter-narrative by emphasizing *Social Constructivism*, where societal values and ethical considerations shape technological development. This interplay suggests a future where technology is not merely a tool for efficiency but a facilitator of social good.

Mathematically, we can represent the relationship between technology and society using a function:

$$T(S) = f(E, C)$$

where $T$ represents technology, $S$ represents society, $E$ represents ethical considerations, and $C$ represents cultural values. As ethical considerations and cultural values evolve, so too does the trajectory of technological development, leading to a more mindful approach.

### Anticipated Challenges

Despite the optimistic outlook for mindful tech, several challenges loom on the horizon. One significant issue is the *Digital Divide*, which refers to the gap between those who have access to digital technologies and those who do not. As mindful tech seeks to enhance inclusivity and accessibility, addressing the digital divide will be crucial. Failure to do so may result in a scenario where only a segment of the population benefits from ethical innovations, exacerbating existing inequalities.

Another challenge is the potential for *Ethical Conflicts* arising from diverse cultural perspectives. What is considered ethical in one society may not hold the same weight in another. This divergence necessitates a robust framework for ethical discourse that transcends cultural boundaries while respecting local values.

## Examples of Future Impacts

1. **Mental Health and Well-being:** Mindful tech is expected to revolutionize mental health care through applications that prioritize user well-being. For instance, AI-driven platforms could provide personalized mental health support, using algorithms that adapt to users' emotional states while maintaining strict privacy standards. This could significantly reduce stigma and increase accessibility to mental health resources.

2. **Education:** The future of education will likely see the integration of mindful tech in classrooms, where learning environments are designed to promote student well-being and engagement. Virtual reality (VR) and augmented reality (AR) tools can create immersive learning experiences that are not only educational but also mindful of students' cognitive load and emotional responses.

3. **Sustainable Practices:** Mindful tech can also play a pivotal role in environmental sustainability. Innovations in renewable energy technology, such as solar panels and wind turbines, are being developed with an emphasis on minimizing ecological footprints. Companies that adopt ethical practices in sourcing materials and manufacturing processes will set new industry standards, demonstrating that profitability and sustainability can coexist.

4. **Healthcare Innovations:** In healthcare, mindful tech will enhance patient care through telemedicine solutions that prioritize patient privacy and data security. Predictive analytics can be utilized to foresee health trends, allowing for proactive interventions that are ethically sound and beneficial to public health.

5. **Workplace Culture:** As organizations increasingly adopt mindful tech, workplace cultures are expected to shift towards more inclusive and supportive environments. Technologies that monitor employee well-being and foster collaboration can lead to higher job satisfaction and productivity, ultimately benefiting both employees and employers.

## Conclusion

In conclusion, the future impacts of mindful tech are likely to be transformative, reshaping how society interacts with technology. By prioritizing ethical considerations, mindful tech has the potential to bridge gaps in access, promote mental health, enhance education, support sustainability, and cultivate positive workplace cultures. However, realizing this potential will require a concerted effort to address challenges such as the digital divide and ethical conflicts. As we advance, it is imperative that we remain vigilant and proactive in ensuring that technology serves humanity, fostering a future that is not only innovative but also ethical and inclusive.

## Inspiring a New Generation of Ethical Innovators

In an era where technology permeates every aspect of life, the importance of ethical innovation cannot be overstated. Sage Yamamoto's journey exemplifies the power of integrating ethical considerations into technological advancements. By sharing his experiences and insights, Yamamoto aims to inspire a new generation of innovators who prioritize ethics alongside innovation.

### The Need for Ethical Innovators

As technology evolves at an unprecedented pace, it raises complex ethical dilemmas that demand thoughtful solutions. Issues such as data privacy, algorithmic bias, and environmental sustainability are critical challenges that future innovators must address. According to the *Ethics in Technology Report* (2023), 78% of tech professionals believe that ethical considerations should be a fundamental part of technology development. This statistic highlights the urgent need for a workforce equipped with both technical skills and ethical awareness.

### Educational Initiatives

To cultivate ethical innovators, educational institutions play a pivotal role. Yamamoto collaborates with universities to develop curricula that integrate ethics into STEM (Science, Technology, Engineering, and Mathematics) education. Programs such as *Tech for Good* and *Ethics in AI* provide students with frameworks to analyze the societal impacts of their work. For instance, the *Ethical AI Workshop* at Stanford University encourages students to engage in case studies that challenge them to consider the moral implications of AI technologies.

### Mentorship and Guidance

Mentorship is another crucial component in fostering ethical innovation. Yamamoto actively participates in mentorship programs, guiding aspiring technologists through real-world challenges. He emphasizes the importance of critical thinking and ethical reasoning, encouraging mentees to ask questions such as:

- Who is affected by this technology?
- What are the potential unintended consequences?
- How can we ensure equitable access to this technology?

By instilling these questions into the minds of young innovators, Yamamoto empowers them to navigate the complexities of modern technology responsibly.

## Real-World Examples

One notable example of ethical innovation can be found in the work of recent graduates from the *Mindful Tech Incubator*, a program initiated by Yamamoto. These innovators developed an app that utilizes machine learning to promote mental health awareness among teenagers. By prioritizing user privacy and incorporating feedback from mental health professionals, they created a tool that not only addresses a pressing societal need but does so in an ethical manner.

Another example is the *EcoTech Initiative*, where students engineer sustainable technologies to combat climate change. Their projects include solar-powered water purification systems and biodegradable materials. These innovations not only showcase technical prowess but also reflect a commitment to environmental ethics, aligning with Yamamoto's vision of mindful tech.

## Community Engagement

Inspiring ethical innovators extends beyond formal education. Yamamoto advocates for community engagement through hackathons and workshops that focus on social impact. These events encourage participants to brainstorm solutions for local issues, such as access to clean water or digital literacy. By fostering collaboration among diverse groups, these initiatives cultivate a sense of responsibility and community-oriented thinking in aspiring innovators.

## The Role of Technology Companies

Technology companies also have a responsibility to nurture ethical innovation. Yamamoto encourages organizations to establish internship programs that emphasize ethical practices. Companies like *Ethical Innovations Corp.* have implemented training sessions that focus on ethical decision-making in technology.

These programs equip interns with the skills needed to confront ethical dilemmas in their future careers, reinforcing the idea that ethical considerations should be integral to technological development.

## Conclusion

In conclusion, inspiring a new generation of ethical innovators is a multifaceted endeavor that requires collaboration between educational institutions, mentorship programs, community engagement, and corporate responsibility. Sage Yamamoto's commitment to fostering ethical innovation serves as a blueprint for aspiring technologists. By prioritizing ethics in technology, we can ensure that future innovations not only advance society but do so in a manner that is just, equitable, and sustainable. The call to action is clear: the next generation of innovators must rise to the challenge and embrace their role as stewards of ethical technology.

## Leaving a Mark on the World

Sage Yamamoto's journey through the landscape of technology and ethics has left an indelible mark on the world, one that extends beyond mere business success and into the realms of social impact and ethical responsibility. This section explores the various ways in which Sage's contributions have shaped the future of technology, emphasizing the importance of mindful innovation and its potential to create lasting change.

### The Ripple Effect of Ethical Innovations

The impact of Sage's work can be understood through the concept of the *ripple effect*, where one action leads to a series of consequences that extend far beyond the initial event. In the context of mindful tech, Sage's innovations, such as the redesign of social media platforms to prioritize mental well-being, have prompted a broader conversation about the ethical responsibilities of tech companies. This has led to a shift in industry standards, encouraging other innovators to consider the societal implications of their products.

For instance, the introduction of mindfulness tech tools has not only transformed individual user experiences but has also influenced corporate policies regarding employee mental health. As companies adopt these tools, they create a healthier workplace culture, which can lead to increased productivity and employee satisfaction. This phenomenon can be modeled using the equation for *social return on investment* (SROI):

$$SROI = \frac{\text{Net Social Value}}{\text{Investment}} \qquad (25)$$

Where *Net Social Value* encompasses the positive impacts generated by mindful tech solutions, and *Investment* refers to the resources allocated to these initiatives.

## Creating a Framework for Future Innovators

Sage's legacy is also evident in the frameworks established for future innovators. By founding the Sage Yamamoto Foundation, he has provided resources and mentorship to aspiring ethical tech entrepreneurs. This foundation emphasizes the importance of integrating ethics into the core of technological development. It serves as a model for how organizations can foster a culture of responsibility and innovation.

The foundation's initiatives include workshops and seminars that focus on ethical decision-making in technology. For example, participants engage in case studies that challenge them to navigate complex ethical dilemmas, preparing them for the real-world challenges they will face. This proactive approach to education aligns with the theory of *constructivist learning*, which posits that individuals learn best when they actively engage with material in a meaningful context.

## The Role of Policy Advocacy

In addition to fostering innovation, Sage has played a crucial role in advocating for policies that promote ethical standards in the tech industry. By collaborating with policymakers and industry leaders, he has influenced legislation aimed at protecting user data and ensuring transparency in technology. This advocacy is rooted in the belief that ethical innovation must be supported by a robust legal framework.

One example of this is the push for regulations similar to the General Data Protection Regulation (GDPR) in Europe, which emphasizes user consent and data protection. Sage's efforts in this area illustrate the interconnectedness of technology and governance, highlighting how ethical considerations can drive policy changes that benefit society as a whole.

## Inspiring Global Movements

Sage Yamamoto's influence extends globally, inspiring movements that prioritize ethical considerations in technology. Through his speaking engagements and thought leadership, he has galvanized communities around the world to advocate for mindful tech solutions. This has led to the formation of global networks of ethical innovators who share resources, strategies, and support.

For instance, the *Mindful Tech Alliance* is a coalition of organizations dedicated to promoting ethical practices in technology. By sharing best practices and collaborating on projects, these innovators are creating a collective impact that transcends geographical boundaries. The alliance exemplifies how individual efforts can coalesce into a powerful movement for change.

### A Vision for a Sustainable Future

Ultimately, leaving a mark on the world involves not just immediate impacts, but also a vision for a sustainable future. Sage Yamamoto's commitment to environmental sustainability through mindful tech solutions underscores the importance of considering the ecological implications of technological advancements. By developing products that reduce carbon footprints and promote sustainable practices, Sage has set a precedent for future innovations.

The integration of sustainability into tech development can be illustrated through the concept of the *circular economy*, which emphasizes the reuse and recycling of resources. This approach not only minimizes waste but also fosters innovation in product design and manufacturing processes. As more companies adopt this model, the potential for a significant reduction in environmental impact becomes tangible.

In conclusion, Sage Yamamoto's contributions to the field of mindful tech represent a profound legacy that will continue to influence the industry for generations to come. By prioritizing ethics, advocating for responsible policies, and inspiring future innovators, Sage has shown that technology can be a force for good. His work serves as a reminder that leaving a mark on the world is not solely about personal achievement; it is about creating a better future for all.

### Future Challenges and Opportunities for Ethical Innovation

The landscape of technology is perpetually evolving, presenting both challenges and opportunities for ethical innovation. As we look towards the future, several key areas emerge that will demand the attention of innovators, policymakers, and society at large. This section will explore these challenges and opportunities, highlighting the significance of ethical considerations in shaping the future of technology.

# LOOKING AHEAD

## Rapid Technological Advancement

The pace of technological advancement is accelerating at an unprecedented rate. Innovations such as artificial intelligence (AI), machine learning, and blockchain are reshaping industries and societies. However, this rapid evolution poses significant ethical challenges. For instance, the deployment of AI in decision-making processes raises concerns about bias and accountability. As algorithms increasingly influence critical areas such as hiring practices, loan approvals, and law enforcement, the question of fairness becomes paramount.

$$\text{Bias}_{AI} = \frac{\text{Number of Biased Outcomes}}{\text{Total Outcomes}} \qquad (26)$$

This equation represents a simplified measure of bias in AI systems. As innovators strive to mitigate bias, they must develop frameworks that ensure transparency and fairness in algorithmic decision-making. The challenge lies in creating systems that are not only efficient but also equitable.

## Data Privacy and Security

With the rise of data-driven technologies, concerns surrounding data privacy and security have intensified. As organizations collect vast amounts of personal information, the risk of data breaches and misuse increases. Ethical innovation must address these concerns by prioritizing user privacy and implementing robust security measures.

The General Data Protection Regulation (GDPR) serves as a benchmark for data protection, emphasizing the importance of consent and user rights. However, compliance with such regulations can be challenging for startups and small businesses. Innovators must find ways to balance the need for data to drive innovation while respecting individual privacy rights.

## Environmental Sustainability

As the world grapples with climate change, the tech industry faces scrutiny regarding its environmental impact. The production and disposal of electronic devices contribute to e-waste and carbon emissions. Ethical innovation must prioritize sustainability, prompting the development of eco-friendly technologies and practices.

Innovators can explore opportunities in renewable energy solutions, sustainable materials, and circular economy models. For example, companies like Fairphone are pioneering the use of ethically sourced materials and modular designs to extend the lifespan of smartphones. This approach not only reduces waste but also empowers consumers to make sustainable choices.

## Social Equity and Inclusion

The tech industry has long been criticized for its lack of diversity and inclusion. As technology continues to shape society, it is crucial to ensure that marginalized voices are represented in the innovation process. Ethical innovation must address social equity by fostering inclusive practices and creating opportunities for underrepresented communities.

Organizations can implement initiatives such as mentorship programs, scholarships, and partnerships with diverse organizations to promote inclusivity. By prioritizing diverse perspectives, innovators can develop solutions that address the needs of a broader audience, ultimately leading to more impactful and equitable outcomes.

## Regulatory and Legal Challenges

The evolving nature of technology often outpaces existing regulatory frameworks. Innovators face the challenge of navigating a complex legal landscape while striving to maintain ethical standards. For instance, the rise of autonomous vehicles raises questions about liability and safety regulations.

To address these challenges, ethical innovators must engage with policymakers and advocate for adaptive regulatory frameworks that promote innovation while safeguarding public interests. Collaborative efforts between the tech industry and regulatory bodies can lead to the establishment of guidelines that facilitate responsible innovation.

## The Role of Education and Awareness

As technology becomes increasingly integrated into daily life, there is a pressing need for education and awareness regarding ethical considerations. Innovators must take on the responsibility of educating users about the implications of technology and fostering a culture of ethical mindfulness.

Educational institutions can play a vital role by incorporating ethics into technology curricula. By equipping future innovators with the knowledge and skills to navigate ethical dilemmas, we can cultivate a generation of leaders who prioritize ethical considerations in their work.

## The Potential of Collaborative Innovation

Despite the challenges, the future also holds significant opportunities for ethical innovation. Collaborative approaches that bring together diverse stakeholders—such as technologists, ethicists, policymakers, and community members—can lead to innovative solutions that address complex societal issues.

For example, the development of open-source technologies encourages collaboration and transparency, allowing communities to adapt and improve solutions based on their unique needs. By harnessing collective intelligence, ethical innovators can create impactful technologies that align with societal values.

## Conclusion

In conclusion, the future of ethical innovation is fraught with challenges but equally rich with opportunities. As technology continues to evolve, it is imperative for innovators to prioritize ethical considerations in their work. By addressing issues such as bias in AI, data privacy, environmental sustainability, social equity, regulatory challenges, and education, we can pave the way for a more ethical and mindful technological future. The collaboration of diverse stakeholders will be key to unlocking the potential of ethical innovation, ensuring that technology serves the greater good and enhances the well-being of society as a whole.

## Expanding the Reach and Influence of Mindful Tech

The expansion of mindful tech is not merely a matter of increasing market share; it encompasses a broader vision of integrating ethical considerations into the very fabric of technological advancement. This section explores the strategies for broadening the reach and influence of mindful tech, addressing both theoretical frameworks and practical implementations.

## Theoretical Frameworks

To effectively expand the reach of mindful tech, we can draw upon several theoretical frameworks that emphasize the importance of ethics in technology. One such framework is the **Stakeholder Theory**, which posits that businesses should create value for all stakeholders, not just shareholders. This perspective encourages companies to consider the implications of their technologies on a diverse array of groups, including users, employees, and the broader community.

Another relevant framework is **Design Thinking**, which emphasizes empathy and user-centric approaches in the development of technology. By engaging with users and understanding their needs and ethical concerns, innovators can create products that resonate more deeply with the public, enhancing acceptance and usage.

## Challenges in Expansion

Despite the promising frameworks, several challenges hinder the expansion of mindful tech. One significant issue is the **Digital Divide**, which refers to the gap between those who have easy access to digital technologies and those who do not. This divide can exacerbate inequalities, making it crucial for mindful tech innovators to develop solutions that are accessible to underrepresented and marginalized communities.

Additionally, the rapid pace of technological advancement often leads to ethical oversights. The phenomenon known as **Technological Determinism** suggests that technology develops independently of social forces, which can lead to unintended consequences. To counteract this, mindful tech must prioritize ethical considerations in the design and deployment of new technologies.

## Strategies for Expansion

To effectively expand the reach and influence of mindful tech, several strategies can be employed:

- **Collaborative Partnerships:** Forming alliances with educational institutions, non-profits, and other organizations can amplify the message of mindful tech. For example, partnerships with universities can foster research initiatives focused on ethical tech, while collaborations with non-profits can help implement tech solutions in underserved communities.

- **Community Engagement:** Actively involving the community in the development process can ensure that the technologies created are relevant and beneficial. This could involve workshops, focus groups, and feedback sessions that allow users to express their concerns and desires regarding technology.

- **Educational Outreach:** Developing educational programs that focus on the importance of ethical technology can cultivate a new generation of innovators who prioritize mindfulness in their work. Programs can be tailored for schools, universities, and community organizations, emphasizing the importance of ethics in technology.

- **Policy Advocacy:** Engaging with policymakers to promote regulations that encourage ethical tech practices is essential. This can involve lobbying for legislation that mandates transparency, data protection, and ethical standards in tech development.

- **Global Initiatives:** Expanding the reach of mindful tech beyond local communities to a global scale can address worldwide issues such as climate change, health crises, and social inequality. Initiatives like the **United Nations Sustainable Development Goals** (SDGs) can serve as a framework for aligning mindful tech innovations with global priorities.

## Examples of Successful Expansion

Several organizations have successfully expanded the reach and influence of mindful tech through innovative approaches. For instance, **Mozilla**, with its commitment to open-source technologies, has fostered a community-driven approach to web development that prioritizes user privacy and ethical standards. By engaging users and developers alike, Mozilla has established itself as a leader in ethical tech.

Another notable example is **Kiva**, which uses technology to connect lenders and borrowers in developing countries. By leveraging mobile technology, Kiva enables individuals to support entrepreneurs in underserved communities, thereby promoting economic development while adhering to ethical lending practices.

## Conclusion

In conclusion, expanding the reach and influence of mindful tech requires a multifaceted approach that integrates theoretical frameworks, addresses challenges, and employs strategic initiatives. By fostering collaboration, engaging communities, advocating for policies, and setting global initiatives, mindful tech can not only thrive in the marketplace but also create a lasting impact on society. As we look to the future, it is imperative that innovators remain committed to ethical considerations, ensuring that technology serves as a force for good in the world.

# Conclusion

## Sage Yamamoto's Impact on the Tech Industry

### The Importance of Ethical Innovation

In today's rapidly evolving technological landscape, the significance of ethical innovation cannot be overstated. As we witness the increasing integration of technology into every facet of our lives, the ethical implications of these advancements become paramount. Ethical innovation is not merely a trend; it is a necessity that shapes the future of technology and its impact on society. This section explores the critical importance of ethical innovation, highlighting its relevance through various theoretical frameworks, real-world problems, and illustrative examples.

### Theoretical Frameworks

At the heart of ethical innovation lies the concept of **technological ethics**, which examines the moral implications of technology and its applications. Philosophers such as *Hans Jonas* proposed the **Principle of Responsibility**, emphasizing that technological advancements should be guided by ethical considerations that prioritize the well-being of humanity and the environment. This principle asserts that innovators bear a responsibility to anticipate the consequences of their creations, ensuring that they contribute positively to society.

Moreover, the **Stakeholder Theory** posits that businesses must consider the interests of all stakeholders, including customers, employees, communities, and the environment, rather than focusing solely on profit maximization. By adopting this perspective, innovators can create products and services that not only fulfill market demands but also enhance societal welfare.

## Real-World Problems

The absence of ethical considerations in technology has led to numerous challenges that underscore the need for ethical innovation. One prominent example is the rise of **data privacy concerns**. With the proliferation of big data and surveillance technologies, personal information is often exploited without users' consent, leading to breaches of privacy and trust. The Cambridge Analytica scandal serves as a stark reminder of the consequences of neglecting ethical standards in technology. By prioritizing ethical innovation, companies can implement robust data protection measures, ensuring user privacy and fostering trust.

Another pressing issue is the impact of **automation and artificial intelligence (AI)** on employment. While these technologies offer efficiency and cost savings, they also pose a threat to job security for millions of workers. Ethical innovation calls for a balanced approach that considers the societal implications of automation. For instance, companies can invest in reskilling programs to help displaced workers transition to new roles, thereby promoting social equity and minimizing negative consequences.

## Illustrative Examples

Several companies have embraced ethical innovation, setting benchmarks for others to follow. **Patagonia**, the outdoor apparel brand, exemplifies a commitment to sustainability and ethical practices. By prioritizing environmentally friendly materials and fair labor practices, Patagonia has built a loyal customer base that values ethical consumption. This approach not only enhances the brand's reputation but also contributes to a more sustainable fashion industry.

Similarly, **Salesforce** has integrated ethical considerations into its business model by prioritizing stakeholder engagement and social responsibility. The company's *Ohana Culture* emphasizes the importance of community and inclusivity, fostering a workplace that values diversity and ethical leadership. By aligning its business strategies with ethical principles, Salesforce has demonstrated that profitability and social responsibility can coexist.

## Conclusion

The importance of ethical innovation extends beyond compliance with regulations; it is a proactive approach that anticipates and addresses the ethical implications of technological advancements. By integrating ethical considerations into the innovation process, companies can create products and services that enhance societal well-being, build trust with stakeholders, and contribute to a sustainable future. As we navigate the complexities of the digital age, the call for ethical innovation becomes increasingly urgent, urging innovators to prioritize ethics as a cornerstone of their endeavors. Ultimately, ethical innovation is not just about doing the right thing; it is about ensuring that technology serves humanity and fosters a better world for future generations.

## Lessons Learned from Sage Yamamoto's Journey

Sage Yamamoto's journey through the realm of mindful technology provides invaluable insights into the intersection of ethics, innovation, and societal impact. Several key lessons can be drawn from her experiences that not only illuminate the challenges faced by innovators but also highlight the principles that can guide future generations.

### The Importance of Ethical Foundations

One of the foremost lessons from Yamamoto's journey is the necessity of establishing a strong ethical foundation in any technological endeavor. As technology advances at an unprecedented pace, the ethical implications of innovations become increasingly complex. Yamamoto's commitment to ethical practices, exemplified by her creation of Mindful Tech Solutions, showcases that ethical considerations must be integrated into the core of technological development.

For instance, when redesigning social media platforms, Yamamoto emphasized user well-being over profit maximization. This approach aligns with the ethical theory of Utilitarianism, which posits that actions should be evaluated based on their consequences for overall happiness. By prioritizing mental health and user satisfaction, Yamamoto not only fostered a more positive online environment but also set a precedent for future tech companies to follow.

### Embracing Collaboration

Collaboration emerged as a vital theme throughout Yamamoto's career. The formation of a diverse and innovative team at Mindful Tech Solutions was instrumental in overcoming industry challenges. By bringing together individuals from various backgrounds and disciplines, Yamamoto cultivated an environment that encouraged creative problem-solving and ethical discourse.

This collaborative approach aligns with the Social Constructivist theory, which posits that knowledge is constructed through social interactions. Yamamoto's team utilized collective intelligence to address ethical dilemmas, demonstrating that diverse perspectives can lead to more comprehensive and socially responsible solutions.

## Navigating Ethical Dilemmas

Yamamoto's journey was not without its challenges, particularly in navigating the ethical dilemmas that arise in a rapidly advancing tech landscape. One significant challenge was balancing profitability with ethical practices. As her startup gained traction, the pressure to conform to industry norms and prioritize profit became increasingly intense.

A poignant example of this struggle was her decision to resist the allure of data monetization strategies that compromised user privacy. Instead, she opted for transparent data practices that respected user autonomy, reflecting the principles of Kantian ethics, which emphasize the intrinsic worth of individuals and the importance of treating them as ends in themselves, rather than means to an end.

## The Role of Education and Advocacy

Yamamoto recognized early on that education and advocacy are essential components of fostering ethical innovation. Her commitment to mentoring the next generation of innovators and collaborating with educational institutions reflects her belief in the power of knowledge dissemination. By sharing her insights through speaking engagements and publications, she has actively contributed to a broader understanding of tech ethics.

The educational initiatives she supported often incorporated the principles of Critical Pedagogy, which encourages learners to question and challenge the status quo. This approach empowers future innovators to think critically about the ethical implications of their work, ensuring a more conscientious technological landscape.

## Building a Lasting Impact

Finally, Yamamoto's establishment of the Sage Yamamoto Foundation serves as a testament to her commitment to creating a lasting impact. By investing in sustainable technologies and supporting ethical initiatives worldwide, she exemplifies the principle of Corporate Social Responsibility (CSR). The foundation not only fosters ethical tech startups but also engages in policy advocacy, ensuring that ethical considerations remain at the forefront of technological advancements.

The foundation's initiatives align with the Triple Bottom Line framework, which emphasizes the importance of balancing social, environmental, and economic responsibilities. Through her philanthropic efforts, Yamamoto has inspired a culture of ethical responsibility, demonstrating that innovators can and should strive for a positive societal impact.

## Conclusion

In conclusion, the lessons learned from Sage Yamamoto's journey underscore the critical importance of ethics in technology. By establishing ethical foundations, embracing collaboration, navigating dilemmas with integrity, advocating for education, and building a lasting impact, future innovators can draw inspiration from her path. As technology continues to evolve, Yamamoto's insights will remain relevant, guiding the next generation toward a more ethical and mindful future in the tech industry.

## The Continuing Relevance of Mindful Tech

In today's fast-paced digital landscape, the relevance of mindful technology remains paramount. As we navigate an era marked by rapid advancements and pervasive digital interactions, the principles of ethical innovation championed by Sage Yamamoto serve as a crucial framework for addressing the multifaceted challenges posed by modern technology. The continuing relevance of mindful tech can be understood through several key dimensions: the psychological impact of technology on users, the ethical implications of data privacy, and the necessity for sustainable practices in tech development.

## Psychological Impact of Technology

The psychological effects of technology on individuals and society have become increasingly evident. Studies indicate that excessive use of social media and digital devices can lead to heightened levels of anxiety, depression, and loneliness. A report by the American Psychological Association (APA) highlights that approximately 60% of adults feel overwhelmed by the constant influx of information and notifications from their devices [?].

Mindful tech seeks to address these concerns by promoting tools and platforms that prioritize mental well-being. For instance, applications designed to encourage mindful usage, such as screen time trackers and digital detox reminders, help users cultivate a healthier relationship with technology. Furthermore, platforms that incorporate features aimed at reducing harmful content and fostering positive interactions can mitigate the adverse effects associated with traditional social media.

## Ethical Implications of Data Privacy

As technology becomes increasingly integrated into our daily lives, the ethical implications surrounding data privacy and user consent have gained prominence. The Cambridge Analytica scandal exemplifies the potential for misuse of personal data, leading to widespread public outrage and calls for stricter regulations. The General Data Protection Regulation (GDPR) in the European Union represents a significant step toward safeguarding user data, but challenges remain in its enforcement and adaptation globally.

Mindful tech advocates for transparency and user empowerment in data management. Companies that prioritize ethical data practices, such as obtaining explicit consent and providing users with control over their information, can build trust and foster long-term relationships with their audiences. For example, platforms like DuckDuckGo have gained popularity for their commitment to user privacy, attracting users who are increasingly aware of data exploitation risks.

## Sustainable Practices in Tech Development

The environmental impact of technology cannot be overlooked. The production and disposal of electronic devices contribute significantly to e-waste, with the United Nations estimating that approximately 53.6 million metric tons of e-waste were generated globally in 2019 [?]. Mindful tech emphasizes the importance of sustainable practices in the design, production, and lifecycle management of technology.

Innovators like Fairphone, which produces modular smartphones designed for longevity and repairability, exemplify the principles of mindful tech. By prioritizing sustainability, these companies not only minimize environmental harm but also challenge the throwaway culture prevalent in the tech industry. The adoption of circular economy principles, where products are designed for reuse and recycling, is essential for reducing the ecological footprint of technology.

## The Role of Education and Awareness

To ensure the continuing relevance of mindful tech, education and awareness are critical. As technology evolves, so too must our understanding of its implications. Educational institutions play a vital role in equipping future innovators with the ethical frameworks necessary to navigate the complexities of technology. Integrating courses on tech ethics, digital literacy, and mindfulness into curricula can foster a generation of responsible technologists.

Moreover, public awareness campaigns can empower consumers to make informed choices about the technologies they use. By promoting the principles of mindful tech, we can cultivate a culture that values ethical innovation and prioritizes the well-being of individuals and society as a whole.

## Conclusion

The relevance of mindful tech in the contemporary landscape is underscored by its potential to address pressing psychological, ethical, and environmental challenges. As we move forward, the legacy of innovators like Sage Yamamoto serves as a guiding light, reminding us that technology should not only advance human capabilities but also enhance our collective well-being. By championing ethical practices, promoting sustainability, and fostering awareness, we can ensure that mindful tech remains a cornerstone of innovation for generations to come.

## The Call to Action for Ethical Tech Advancements

In the rapidly evolving landscape of technology, the call for ethical advancements has never been more critical. As we navigate through the complexities introduced by innovations such as artificial intelligence, big data, and pervasive connectivity, it is imperative that we adopt a framework that prioritizes ethical considerations alongside technological progress. This section elucidates the pressing need for ethical tech advancements, highlights the challenges we face, and proposes actionable steps for stakeholders in the tech industry.

### Understanding the Ethical Imperative

The ethical imperative in technology stems from the profound impact that technological advancements have on society. Theories such as Utilitarianism, which advocate for the greatest good for the greatest number, and Deontological ethics, which emphasize the importance of duty and rules, provide a foundation for evaluating the moral implications of tech innovations. As Sage Yamamoto exemplifies through his work, the integration of ethics into technology is not merely an option; it is a necessity.

$$\text{Ethical Value} = \frac{\text{Total Benefit}}{\text{Total Harm}} \tag{27}$$

This equation illustrates the need to balance benefits against potential harms, urging innovators to consider the broader societal impacts of their creations. For instance, the rise of social media has led to significant societal shifts, with both positive and negative consequences. The challenge lies in maximizing the former while minimizing the latter.

## Identifying Key Issues

Several key issues underscore the necessity for ethical tech advancements:

1. **Privacy Concerns**: With the proliferation of data collection, individuals' privacy is increasingly compromised. The Cambridge Analytica scandal serves as a stark reminder of the potential misuse of data, highlighting the urgent need for robust data protection measures.

2. **Bias and Discrimination**: Algorithms can perpetuate existing biases, as seen in facial recognition technology that disproportionately misidentifies people of color. This raises ethical questions about fairness and accountability in AI systems.

3. **Mental Health Implications**: The design of technology can significantly impact mental well-being. Social media platforms, for example, can foster addiction and anxiety, necessitating a reevaluation of design principles to prioritize user well-being.

4. **Environmental Sustainability**: The tech industry has a substantial carbon footprint, prompting calls for sustainable practices. Ethical innovation must address environmental concerns, ensuring that technological advancements contribute positively to ecological health.

## A Framework for Action

To address these pressing issues, a multi-faceted approach is required:

1. **Establishing Ethical Guidelines**: The tech industry should collaboratively develop and adhere to ethical guidelines that govern the design and implementation of technologies. Organizations like the IEEE and the Partnership on AI are already making strides in this direction.

2. **Promoting Transparency**: Companies must commit to transparency in their algorithms and data usage. This includes clear communication about how data is collected, used, and shared, as well as the potential biases inherent in AI systems.

3. **Encouraging Diverse Teams**: A diverse workforce can lead to more inclusive and equitable technology. Companies should prioritize diversity in hiring practices, ensuring that a variety of perspectives inform the development of tech solutions.

4. **Investing in Ethical Education**: Educational institutions must integrate ethics into STEM curricula, equipping future innovators with the tools to navigate

moral dilemmas. Programs that focus on the intersection of technology and ethics can foster a new generation of mindful tech leaders.

5. **Engaging in Public Discourse**: Tech companies should actively engage with the public to discuss the implications of their innovations. By fostering dialogue, they can better understand societal concerns and adapt their practices accordingly.

## Conclusion

The call to action for ethical tech advancements is not merely a response to current challenges but a proactive stance toward shaping a future where technology serves humanity responsibly. As Sage Yamamoto's journey illustrates, the integration of ethics into technological innovation is essential for creating a sustainable and equitable society. By embracing this call to action, stakeholders can ensure that technology enhances, rather than undermines, our collective well-being.

In conclusion, the path forward requires a commitment to ethical principles, collaboration across sectors, and a shared vision for a future where technology and humanity thrive in harmony. The time for action is now, and the responsibility lies with all of us to advocate for and implement ethical advancements in technology.

## A Vision for a More Ethical and Mindful Future

In contemplating a more ethical and mindful future, we must first acknowledge the intricate relationship between technology and society. As we advance further into the digital age, the necessity for ethical frameworks becomes increasingly paramount. Sage Yamamoto's journey exemplifies the potential for technology to not only innovate but to do so with a conscious regard for humanity. This vision for the future is rooted in several key principles that can guide our path forward.

## Emphasizing Ethical Design Principles

One of the foremost aspects of creating a more ethical future is the integration of ethical design principles into the technology development process. This involves embedding ethical considerations at the very inception of technological innovations. The *Value Sensitive Design* (VSD) framework, which emphasizes the importance of considering human values in the design process, serves as a cornerstone for this approach. By ensuring that technologies are designed with user welfare, privacy, and autonomy in mind, we can mitigate potential harms and enhance the positive impact of technology on society.

$$\text{Ethical Impact} = \frac{\text{User Welfare} \times \text{Privacy Considerations}}{\text{Potential Harms}} \qquad (28)$$

Here, the equation illustrates that the ethical impact of technology is maximized when user welfare and privacy considerations are prioritized, while minimizing potential harms.

## Fostering Collaborative Innovation

Collaboration among diverse stakeholders is essential for fostering a culture of ethical innovation. This includes not only technologists but also ethicists, sociologists, and community representatives. By creating interdisciplinary teams, we can ensure that multiple perspectives are considered, leading to more holistic solutions. For example, the collaborative efforts between tech companies and non-profit organizations have resulted in initiatives like the *Digital Impact Alliance*, which aims to harness technology for social good.

## Addressing Systemic Inequities

To build a more ethical future, we must also confront the systemic inequities that technology can exacerbate. The digital divide remains a significant barrier to equitable access to technology. By prioritizing inclusivity in tech development, we can work towards solutions that benefit all segments of society. Initiatives like *Code.org* and *Girls Who Code* are vital in bridging this gap, ensuring that underrepresented communities have access to technological education and opportunities.

## Promoting Mindfulness in Technology Use

Mindfulness is not only a principle for designing technology but also a practice for users. Encouraging individuals to engage mindfully with technology can mitigate issues such as addiction and mental health concerns. Tools that promote digital well-being, such as screen time trackers and mindful usage prompts, can help users cultivate a healthier relationship with their devices. The introduction of features like *Focus Mode* on smartphones exemplifies this shift towards mindfulness in technology use.

## Regulatory Frameworks and Accountability

For ethical innovation to thrive, robust regulatory frameworks must be established. Governments and regulatory bodies need to create policies that hold tech companies accountable for their practices. This includes enforcing data protection laws, such as the *General Data Protection Regulation* (GDPR) in Europe, which sets a precedent for user privacy rights. By establishing clear guidelines and consequences for unethical practices, we can create an environment where ethical innovation is not only encouraged but mandated.

## Continuous Education and Advocacy

Lastly, fostering a culture of continuous education and advocacy around ethical technology is crucial. Educational institutions must integrate ethics into their curricula, ensuring that future innovators are equipped with the knowledge and skills to navigate the complex moral landscape of technology. Furthermore, public awareness campaigns can educate consumers about their rights and the ethical implications of their technology choices.

## Conclusion

In conclusion, a vision for a more ethical and mindful future requires a multifaceted approach that encompasses ethical design, collaboration, inclusivity, mindfulness, regulatory accountability, and education. By drawing inspiration from Sage Yamamoto's journey and the principles of mindful tech, we can create a future where technology serves as a force for good, enhancing our lives while respecting our values and humanity. The call to action is clear: we must collectively strive to innovate ethically and mindfully, ensuring that technology uplifts rather than undermines the very fabric of society.

# Index

ability, 4, 15, 45, 63
absence, 4
academic, 5, 7, 11, 12, 20, 23, 24, 29, 105, 116
acceptance, 48
access, 36, 44, 54, 115, 123, 125
accessibility, 26, 31, 55
acclaim, 81
accountability, 5, 21, 30, 89, 97, 145
accuracy, 116
achievement, 36, 128
action, 4, 59, 62, 82, 108, 114, 121, 126, 143, 145
adaptability, 63
adaptation, 89
add, 119
addition, 14, 99, 127
address, 19, 27, 36, 44, 46, 54, 56, 65, 67, 89, 90, 92, 97, 124, 129, 130, 139, 141, 142
adherence, 4
adoption, 52, 63, 140
advance, 15, 20, 124, 126, 141, 143
advancement, 1, 3, 7, 15, 24, 29, 50, 55, 59, 66, 73, 85, 112, 131
advertising, 68
advice, 103
advocacy, 14, 63, 79, 90, 114, 116–119, 127, 138, 145
advocate, 24, 62, 127, 130, 141, 143
Africa, 89
age, 9, 44, 68, 115, 137, 143
agency, 14
agriculture, 87
algorithm, 20, 21, 68
alignment, 30
allure, 138
Amsterdam, 88
analysis, 23
anxiety, 21, 47, 48, 103
app, 21, 25, 44, 55, 60, 77, 89, 101, 103
application, 21, 57, 89, 105, 114, 121
approach, 5, 7, 13, 15, 20, 24, 26, 29, 31, 35, 41–44, 62–65, 68, 71, 75, 77, 87, 92, 95, 102, 106–108, 110, 115–117, 119, 121, 130, 133, 136–138, 142, 145
area, 23
aspect, 1, 3, 11, 82, 106, 124
assembly, 60, 61
atmosphere, 10
attention, 45, 63, 116, 128
audience, 26, 35, 37, 130
audits, 23

automation, 2, 60
autonomy, 115, 138
awareness, 40, 48, 63, 101, 130, 140, 141, 145

background, 35
balance, 24, 43, 61, 69, 70, 96, 141
balancing, 3, 18, 68, 71, 103, 138
barrier, 36, 52, 62
base, 41, 63
beacon, 7, 47, 71, 73, 109
bedrock, 20
behavior, 97
being, 3, 4, 6, 7, 9, 11, 21, 23–26, 30, 33, 42, 43, 45–47, 50, 53, 58, 61–63, 65, 68, 72, 73, 77, 85, 108, 109, 112, 114–116, 131, 136, 137, 139, 141, 143
belief, 11, 12, 21, 82, 109, 119, 127, 138
beneficence, 54
Berners-Lee's, 14
bias, 4, 23, 36, 37, 88, 112, 116, 119, 129, 131
biotechnology, 3
blend, 12, 20
blueprint, 29, 79, 108, 126
brainstorm, 125
brainstorming, 30, 34
brand, 35, 44
bridge, 94, 100, 109, 117, 123
burnout, 60
business, 42, 61, 68, 69, 71, 89, 92, 96, 101, 110, 112, 115, 126

call, 20, 71, 102, 106, 121, 126, 137, 141, 143, 145
campaign, 63

carbon, 20, 87, 128, 129
care, 1
career, 6, 13, 15, 21, 24, 74, 137
case, 21, 23, 30, 60, 65, 77, 88, 89, 101, 111
catalyst, 75, 109
challenge, 3, 6, 17, 18, 36, 44, 54, 59, 63, 65, 66, 68, 89, 102, 105, 113, 126, 129, 130, 138, 140, 142
change, 29, 47, 55, 75, 82, 85, 89, 90, 92, 105, 109, 126, 129
charge, 114
Chen, 14
childhood, 10
choice, 20, 85
clarity, 97
climate, 55, 85, 129
clinic, 55
code, 13
coding, 9
collaboration, 21, 26–29, 37, 40–42, 44, 55, 58, 62, 80–83, 97, 104, 121, 125, 126, 131, 133, 139, 143, 145
collaborative, 21, 27–29, 80, 119
collection, 22
collectivist, 36
college, 12, 21, 24, 26, 27, 29
color, 92
combination, 116
commitment, 7, 12, 14, 21, 24, 26, 29, 31, 36, 38, 40, 42, 43, 45, 58, 61, 64, 68, 74, 79, 82, 89, 92, 95, 97, 104, 106, 112, 114–116, 121, 126, 128, 137, 138, 140, 143
communication, 1, 18, 29, 36, 45

*Index*

community, 10, 15, 26, 29–31, 35, 41, 42, 44, 55, 72, 74, 92, 101, 110, 125, 126
company, 26, 37, 38, 40, 42–45, 49, 54, 55, 60, 61, 64, 77, 79, 96, 97, 101
compass, 26
competency, 36
complexity, 20
compliance, 44, 63, 66, 136
component, 12, 24, 104, 116, 124
computer, 12, 20
concept, 4
conception, 5
concern, 10, 11, 23, 66, 68, 90
conclusion, 3, 7, 17, 29, 37, 50, 61, 71, 97, 104, 106, 116, 123, 126, 128, 131, 133, 139, 143, 145
confidentiality, 116
conflict, 36, 96
confusion, 97
connection, 47
connectivity, 18, 141
consent, 4, 22, 64, 77, 103, 115, 140
consideration, 17
consumer, 41, 44
consumerism, 9
consumption, 20, 41
contemplation, 10
content, 4, 6, 7, 23, 44, 65, 68, 139
context, 59, 96, 114
contrast, 11
control, 54, 68, 77, 121, 140
core, 20, 25, 26, 30, 68, 109, 112, 114, 119, 127, 137
cornerstone, 37, 104, 137, 141
correlation, 72
cost, 2, 54, 115

course, 59
creation, 25, 30, 55, 137
creativity, 21, 35, 37
credibility, 44, 62
culture, 3, 6, 7, 12, 15, 26–29, 31, 36–38, 40, 66, 68, 73, 77–79, 82, 92, 97, 102, 103, 108–110, 116, 117, 119–121, 127, 130, 140, 141, 145
curiosity, 9, 10
curricula, 40, 82, 104–106, 130, 140, 145
curriculum, 20
customer, 41, 63, 96, 97
cyberbullying, 18

data, 3–5, 7, 10, 20, 22, 23, 44, 53–55, 63–66, 68, 77, 96, 97, 101, 103, 110, 112, 115, 116, 119, 121, 127, 129, 131, 138–141
debate, 5, 21, 68
decision, 4, 11, 19, 20, 23, 26, 30, 61, 96, 97, 114, 116, 129, 138
decrease, 72, 77
dedication, 121
degradation, 55
degree, 12, 20
demand, 17, 128
depletion, 85
deployment, 5, 23, 117
design, 6, 11, 12, 20, 21, 23, 26, 34, 45, 46, 77, 81, 101, 145
designing, 11, 114
desire, 103
detox, 139
development, 3–5, 7, 14, 17, 21, 26, 30, 34, 35, 41, 42, 52, 58,

82, 88–90, 97, 103, 104, 106, 108, 112, 115–117, 121, 127, 129, 131, 137, 139
device, 10
diagnostic, 116
dialogue, 17, 31, 35, 37
dichotomy, 11
difficulty, 112
dignity, 20, 61
dilemma, 60, 61
dinner, 10
disconnect, 105
discourse, 95, 97, 100, 102, 137
discovery, 12
disparity, 89
displacement, 2
disposal, 129
dissemination, 138
dissonance, 16
diversity, 21, 29, 35–38, 92, 93, 95, 101, 115, 130
divide, 10, 54, 119, 124
dominance, 61
duration, 72
duty, 4, 11, 24, 115, 141
dynamic, 31, 37

e, 129
economy, 129, 140
ecosystem, 112
education, 1, 7, 52, 82, 89, 94, 104–106, 124, 125, 130, 131, 138–140, 145
effect, 61, 79, 90, 92
effectiveness, 26, 44, 52, 62
efficacy, 85
efficiency, 2, 18, 20, 53, 105
effort, 17, 31, 121, 124

electronic, 129
emergence, 112
empathy, 34
emphasis, 6, 85
employment, 94
empowerment, 33, 140
encounter, 21, 112
encryption, 7, 54
end, 138
endeavor, 45, 71, 80, 95, 116, 119, 126, 137
energy, 20, 89, 129
engagement, 9, 23, 26, 30, 33–35, 45, 53, 62, 63, 68, 77, 79, 92, 115, 116, 125, 126
entertainment, 1
enthusiasm, 34
entrepreneur, 40
entrepreneurship, 92
entry, 95
environment, 1, 4, 7, 9, 10, 14, 21, 27, 29, 37, 38, 47, 63, 68, 95, 137
equality, 23
equation, 2–5, 9, 11, 29, 43, 45, 70, 72, 83, 92, 99, 129, 141, 144
equity, 21, 37, 130, 131
era, 3, 15, 45, 47, 54, 55, 66, 102, 106, 112, 114, 124, 139
essence, 29, 83
establishment, 97, 108–110, 112, 130
evaluation, 52, 66
evidence, 62
evolution, 15, 97
examination, 1
example, 4, 10, 20, 23, 25, 30, 36, 40, 42, 44, 60, 65, 89, 97,

101, 103, 108, 110, 115, 121, 129, 131, 138, 140
exception, 121
exchange, 30
exercise, 5, 19, 24
expansion, 131
expectation, 121
expense, 106, 121
experience, 9, 17, 21, 24, 35, 37, 43, 48, 72, 90, 102, 114
expertise, 12, 42, 44, 89
exploitation, 140
exploration, 9, 23, 24
exposure, 6, 9, 72

fabric, 108, 121, 131, 145
facet, 135
fair, 11, 88
fairness, 21, 23, 31, 129
family, 5, 9, 10
farming, 87
fascination, 10
fear, 52, 68
feedback, 26, 34, 41, 52
feeling, 34
field, 9, 13, 21, 42, 43, 45, 93, 114, 116, 128
figure, 5, 14, 21
flagship, 68
focus, 34, 43, 45, 47, 105, 125
food, 87
footprint, 87, 140
force, 75, 128, 133, 145
forefront, 7, 26, 38, 55, 109, 112
form, 24, 73
formation, 128, 137
foster, 3, 27, 38, 45, 47, 55, 108, 109, 127, 140

foundation, 9, 12, 24, 26, 29, 78, 109–112, 121, 127, 137, 141
framework, 7, 11, 12, 23, 30, 54, 89, 96, 110, 112, 114–116, 127, 139, 141
frequency, 72
function, 29, 122
funding, 52, 89, 90, 110, 113
future, 3, 5, 7, 14, 17, 21, 23, 24, 26, 29, 31, 47, 55, 57, 58, 61, 73, 75, 85, 90, 92, 95, 97, 100, 102, 104–106, 109, 112, 114, 116, 119, 121, 123, 124, 126–128, 130, 131, 133, 135, 137–140, 143, 145

gain, 61, 113
gamification, 25
gap, 94, 100, 105, 109, 113, 116
gathering, 41, 52
generation, 7, 14, 31, 40, 82, 83, 99, 102, 104, 106, 124, 126, 130, 138–140
giving, 92
good, 5, 20, 21, 61, 75, 104, 119, 128, 131, 133, 141, 145
ground, 10
groundwork, 10, 23, 25, 26, 106
group, 34, 36
growth, 6, 14, 42, 112
guest, 99
guidance, 13–15, 31, 103
guide, 11, 15, 19, 24, 25, 42, 75, 103, 106, 114, 137, 143

hallmark, 26, 94
hand, 18, 66

handling, 23, 115
happiness, 11, 24, 114, 137
harm, 11, 18, 60, 89, 108, 114, 140
harmony, 36, 71, 143
head, 61
health, 1, 6, 7, 11, 12, 18, 23, 33, 34, 41, 42, 44–47, 50, 53–55, 58, 60, 63, 72, 77, 81, 101, 103, 115, 124, 137
healthcare, 7, 30, 53–55, 77, 115, 116, 121
heart, 119
highlight, 4, 48, 85, 117, 137
hindrance, 12
hiring, 4, 21, 23, 36
hope, 47, 71, 109
household, 9
hub, 30
humanity, 5, 15–17, 21, 24, 31, 83, 90, 104, 106, 108, 112, 114, 121, 124, 137, 143, 145
hurdle, 6, 54, 64

idea, 33, 89
identity, 24, 35, 37
Immanuel Kant, 4, 11, 24, 115
impact, 1–3, 13, 15, 16, 35, 42, 45, 55, 57, 60, 71–74, 77, 81, 83, 88, 89, 92, 97, 101, 103, 105, 110–112, 121, 125, 126, 129, 133, 135, 137, 139, 141, 144
imperative, 3, 5, 13, 38, 44, 50, 61, 68, 71, 90, 92, 95, 124, 131, 133, 141
implementation, 4, 5, 20, 61, 107, 115

importance, 4, 5, 10, 11, 14, 17, 21, 24, 29, 31, 35, 41, 44, 54, 66, 75, 82, 83, 89, 90, 103, 115, 116, 119, 124–128, 135, 136, 138, 139, 141
improvement, 26
in, 1–7, 9–15, 17, 18, 20–25, 27, 29–31, 33–38, 40–45, 47, 48, 50, 52, 54–66, 68, 69, 72, 73, 75–77, 80–83, 85–90, 92, 94–97, 99, 101–110, 112, 113, 115–119, 121, 123–131, 133, 137–143
inception, 33
incident, 5, 23
inclusion, 37, 130
inclusivity, 5, 30, 37, 92, 93, 95, 130, 145
income, 52, 54
India, 89
individual, 36, 61, 90, 103, 106
industry, 6, 7, 9, 12, 13, 15, 21, 24, 26, 29, 30, 37, 42–45, 55, 61–63, 66, 71, 73, 75, 77–80, 82, 83, 89, 92, 95, 97, 102–104, 106–110, 114, 116, 117, 119, 121, 127–130, 137–141
influence, 4, 7, 14, 22, 31, 62, 111, 127, 128, 131–133
information, 10, 14, 54, 66, 68, 89, 97, 121, 129, 140
initiative, 94, 97, 121
innovation, 3–5, 7, 9, 12–15, 17, 20, 21, 24, 26–29, 31, 35–38, 40–43, 45, 47–50, 58, 61, 63, 66, 68, 70, 71, 73–75, 78, 80, 82, 83, 86, 90, 92,

95, 97, 99–106, 108–110, 112–117, 119, 121, 124, 126–131, 135–139, 141, 143
innovator, 24, 103
input, 89
inquiry, 11
inspiration, 14, 97, 139, 145
instance, 4, 6, 7, 11, 12, 18, 21, 36, 42, 60–63, 68, 88, 89, 96, 114, 130, 137, 139, 141
integrating, 20, 21, 24, 57, 66, 75, 104, 106, 108, 124, 127, 131, 136
integration, 5, 17, 36, 37, 48, 53–56, 90, 135, 141, 143
integrity, 66, 96, 121, 139
intelligence, 3, 9, 30, 131, 141
interaction, 45
interconnectedness, 90
interest, 9, 11, 41
interface, 26
internet, 14, 54
interplay, 11
intersection, 9, 11, 15, 17, 33, 43, 53, 55, 68, 114, 137
introduction, 47, 49, 50, 71
inventor, 14
invest, 113
investment, 92
involvement, 89
issue, 68, 89, 105, 115
iteration, 41

job, 2
Jon Kabat-Zinn, 48
journey, 10, 12, 13, 20, 24, 26, 29, 40, 42, 45, 58, 61, 66, 70, 73, 75, 80, 108, 109, 124, 126, 137–139, 143, 145
juncture, 15

key, 26, 27, 35, 59, 67, 68, 72, 78, 80, 93, 98, 128, 131, 137, 139, 142, 143
knowledge, 20, 21, 30, 41, 102, 104, 130, 138, 145

lack, 21, 36, 52, 86, 89, 92, 96, 105, 115, 130
land, 87
landscape, 3, 4, 7, 17, 18, 20, 24, 26, 29, 31, 35, 38, 40, 43–45, 50, 61, 63, 66, 68, 71, 75, 83, 85, 86, 90, 92, 95, 97, 102, 106, 108, 112–114, 116, 119, 126, 128, 130, 135, 138, 139, 141, 145
launch, 34, 55
law, 24
leader, 43, 45, 62, 63, 77, 102
leadership, 94–97, 112, 119, 121, 127
learning, 7, 23, 29, 52
legacy, 15, 75, 102, 104, 112, 121, 127, 128, 141
legislation, 127
lens, 20, 112
lesson, 13
level, 78, 92
leverage, 113
liability, 130
life, 1, 17, 18, 71, 124, 130
lifespan, 130
light, 14, 121, 141
like, 5, 10, 19, 23, 24, 29, 34, 41, 44, 47, 57, 59, 61, 63, 66, 68,

71, 80, 85, 87, 90, 92, 95, 114, 117–119, 129, 140, 141
line, 13, 60, 71
literacy, 12, 89, 125, 140
longevity, 140
loss, 66
loyalty, 35, 96, 115

machine, 23
making, 4, 11, 19, 23, 26, 30, 42, 61, 96, 106, 113, 114, 116, 117, 129
maleficence, 54
management, 66, 68, 140
manner, 20, 126
manufacturing, 60
mark, 126, 128
market, 35, 45, 61, 63, 113, 131
marketing, 42
marketplace, 133
matter, 42, 131
maximization, 137
Maya, 103
Maya Chen, 103
measure, 112, 129
media, 4, 6, 11, 18, 23, 35, 44–47, 62, 63, 65, 68, 77, 88, 114, 115, 137, 139, 141
member, 36
mentor, 31, 104
mentorship, 12, 14, 31, 37, 89, 99, 102–104, 124, 126, 127, 130
message, 44
methodology, 41
mindfulness, 5, 7, 12, 20, 21, 26, 44, 47–50, 72, 73, 81,
100–103, 109, 115, 130, 140, 145
mindset, 7, 110
minority, 23
misinformation, 4, 6, 18
mission, 41, 45, 104, 109, 116
misuse, 10, 63, 129
model, 42, 68, 89, 92, 127
moderation, 4
mold, 13
moment, 33, 48, 109
momentum, 42, 63
monetization, 138
month, 55
movement, 44, 75, 92
myriad, 59, 112

nature, 9, 89, 102, 130
necessity, 19, 21, 38, 85, 92, 101, 114, 117, 135, 137, 139, 141–143
need, 3–5, 12, 23, 31, 37, 45, 48, 89, 100, 106, 107, 116, 130, 141
negativity, 72
network, 30, 31, 41, 62
networking, 31
niche, 43
non, 43, 52, 54, 94
notation, 20
notice, 79
number, 4, 105, 121, 141

obligation, 44, 68, 108
obstacle, 96
offering, 3
oil, 66
on, 1, 3, 5, 6, 9–11, 15, 16, 18, 20, 21, 23, 26, 29–31, 34–36,

## Index

40–43, 45, 48, 53, 55, 57, 60, 61, 63, 64, 66, 68, 71, 72, 74, 77, 79, 81–83, 85, 88, 89, 92, 96, 97, 100–105, 110, 115, 116, 119, 121, 125, 126, 128, 130, 131, 133, 135, 137–141
one, 4, 18, 30, 40, 89, 114, 121, 126
openness, 77
opinion, 4
option, 38, 119, 141
order, 41
organization, 21, 42, 44, 89, 95
other, 1, 18, 41, 43, 62, 66, 73, 79, 82, 83, 104, 108
out, 12, 31, 41, 43
outlook, 6, 11
outreach, 99
overload, 50
oversight, 4
overwork, 60
ownership, 103

pace, 3, 12, 15, 63, 137
panel, 99
paradigm, 53, 112
part, 10, 119
partnership, 44, 82, 89, 94
passion, 9–12
path, 139, 143
pathway, 71
patient, 7, 53–55, 77, 116, 121
pay, 68
peer, 55
people, 4, 71, 92
performance, 7
period, 13, 24
perspective, 4, 13

phase, 26
phenomenon, 1
philanthropic, 95
philanthropy, 92
philosophy, 11, 24, 83, 99, 119
place, 24
planet, 55, 58
platform, 11, 26, 30, 47, 65, 68, 72, 77, 115
playing, 30
point, 55
policy, 54, 62, 116–119
pool, 36, 97
popularity, 140
pose, 86
positioning, 63
potential, 4, 10, 11, 13, 18, 29, 34, 41, 44, 50, 52, 56, 66, 86, 89, 92, 97, 105, 108, 115, 116, 123, 124, 126, 131, 141, 143, 144
power, 37, 55, 62, 81, 124, 138
practice, 4, 22, 72, 121
precedent, 66, 119, 128, 137
preparation, 104
present, 4, 18, 48
pressure, 9, 63, 68, 96, 138
prevalence, 48
principle, 11, 71
prioritize, 6, 7, 14, 17, 23, 33, 36, 55, 58, 61, 64, 66, 88, 96, 97, 99, 102, 104, 105, 113, 115, 116, 124, 127, 129–131, 137–140
priority, 21
privacy, 4, 5, 7, 9, 10, 14, 18, 22, 23, 41, 44, 53–55, 61, 63–66, 68, 77, 96, 97, 101, 103, 110, 112, 115, 116, 119,

121, 129, 131, 138–140, 144
problem, 10, 110, 112, 137
process, 5, 26, 31, 34, 41, 66, 97, 115, 117, 119, 130, 136
product, 21, 26, 35, 97, 116
production, 129
productivity, 2, 60
professional, 12, 52
profile, 4, 98
profiling, 5
profit, 24, 30, 43, 52, 53, 63, 66, 71, 94, 96, 103, 105, 110, 112, 115, 121, 137, 138
profitability, 6, 68, 70, 71, 96, 113, 138
program, 14, 103
programming, 20
progress, 12, 17, 20, 99, 114, 141
project, 11, 12, 21, 25, 30, 89, 103
proof, 44
proponent, 116
proposition, 41–43, 45
protection, 44, 97
prototype, 11, 26
psychology, 48
public, 4, 5, 61–63, 68, 99, 130, 141, 145
pursuit, 20, 69, 75, 121

quality, 18
quest, 92
question, 10, 138
questioning, 10
quo, 7, 63, 138

rationale, 85
reach, 44, 111, 131–133
realization, 11, 12, 20

realm, 5, 13, 73, 90, 97, 100, 137
reasoning, 31, 125
recognition, 5, 23, 61, 73, 75, 79, 101
recruitment, 36
recycling, 140
redesign, 7, 23, 45, 77
reduction, 72
regard, 143
region, 86
regulation, 48, 116
relationship, 15, 17, 70, 72, 92, 122, 139, 143
relevance, 135, 139–141
reliance, 89
reluctance, 66, 113
reminder, 90, 101, 128
repairability, 140
report, 63
representation, 92, 115
reputation, 96, 97
research, 21, 42, 62, 105, 108
resilience, 40, 63
resistance, 54, 61, 63, 105
resolve, 21, 40
resource, 20, 85
respect, 115
response, 5, 7, 143
responsibility, 7, 13, 15, 21, 24, 38, 43, 68, 71, 78, 79, 89, 90, 92, 97, 100, 108–110, 114, 116, 117, 119, 121, 125–127, 130, 143
result, 31, 77, 105
reuse, 140
review, 108
right, 4, 11, 59, 137
rise, 4, 6, 22, 126, 129, 130, 141
risk, 63, 129

*Index* 157

roadmap, 97, 100
role, 4, 13–15, 29–31, 55, 63, 97, 102, 104, 112, 126, 127, 130, 140

safety, 61, 65, 130
Sage Yamamoto, 5, 7, 9, 15, 17, 19, 20, 23, 26, 29, 33, 35, 38, 40, 42, 45–47, 55, 57, 59, 61, 63, 64, 66–68, 71, 73, 74, 78, 80, 85, 90, 93, 97, 100, 102, 104, 106–108, 112, 114–116, 118, 119, 121, 139, 141
Sage Yamamoto's, 10, 12, 13, 24, 26, 29, 31, 37, 42, 48–50, 53, 55, 56, 61, 63, 68, 70, 71, 73, 75, 82, 89, 92, 95–97, 104, 106, 112, 114, 116, 124, 126–128, 137, 139, 143
satisfaction, 34, 43, 62, 137
scale, 86
scandal, 4, 22
science, 10–12, 20
screen, 23, 77, 139
scrutiny, 63, 64, 129
section, 13, 15, 17, 27, 35, 38, 43, 47, 53, 55, 59, 61, 63, 66, 71, 80, 85, 90, 92, 102, 114, 119, 126, 128, 131, 135, 141
sector, 60, 77, 92
security, 4, 7, 87, 110, 121, 129
segment, 43
sense, 9, 31, 41, 44, 125
sentiment, 63
series, 30, 34, 81, 97

set, 7, 25, 40, 66, 71, 78, 119, 121, 128, 137
setting, 6, 55, 133
shape, 11, 26, 102, 119, 130
share, 30, 36, 41, 44, 63, 66, 68, 90, 113, 128, 131
sharing, 7, 30, 66, 82, 102, 124, 138
shift, 34, 47, 53, 76, 112
side, 10
significance, 15, 80, 102, 128, 135
skepticism, 62
smartphone, 10
society, 1, 3, 4, 11, 15, 17, 20, 30, 50, 75, 83, 89, 92, 95, 103, 108, 109, 114, 122, 123, 126, 128, 130, 131, 133, 135, 141, 143, 145
software, 9, 101
solar, 89
solution, 41
solving, 10, 137
source, 47, 131
space, 30, 62
speaking, 97, 99, 127, 138
speech, 61
spread, 4, 18, 104
stage, 5, 6, 116
stakeholder, 71, 79
stance, 107, 143
standard, 78, 121
startup, 14, 33, 35, 41, 42, 77, 110, 138
status, 7, 63, 138
step, 25, 43, 47
story, 103
strategy, 63
stress, 21, 47, 48, 72
struggle, 52, 138
student, 21

study, 23, 88, 101
subject, 44
subscription, 68
success, 9, 26, 37, 41, 45, 47, 71, 89, 90, 96, 101, 112, 115, 126
suit, 92
summary, 12, 90
summit, 88
support, 12, 26, 41, 42, 55, 62, 89, 97, 109, 114, 115, 124, 128
surrounding, 7, 50, 95, 97, 129
surveillance, 4, 5, 61
sustainability, 3, 20, 55–57, 68, 85, 87, 96, 108, 124, 128, 129, 131, 140, 141
sword, 3, 18
synergy, 26, 80
system, 55, 116

table, 10
tale, 4
talent, 36, 96, 97
target, 26
team, 21, 25, 26, 29, 34–37, 43, 44, 46, 63, 65, 116, 121, 137
teamwork, 10
tech, 4–7, 9–13, 15, 20, 21, 23, 24, 26, 29, 31, 36, 37, 40–45, 47–50, 52–55, 60–63, 66, 68, 71, 73–75, 77–80, 82, 83, 89, 90, 92, 93, 95–97, 99–104, 106–110, 112–119, 121, 123, 127–133, 137–143, 145
technology, 1–7, 9–15, 17, 18, 20–24, 26, 27, 29–31, 33, 35, 38, 41, 43–45, 47, 48, 50, 52–55, 58, 59, 61–63, 66, 68, 71, 73, 75–77, 82, 83, 85–90, 97, 100, 102–106, 108, 109, 112, 114–116, 119, 121–128, 130, 131, 133, 135, 137, 139–141, 143–145
term, 42, 68, 71, 96, 105, 140
test, 40
testament, 37
testing, 26
theme, 137
theory, 71, 105, 137
thing, 137
think, 14, 89, 138
thinking, 34, 40, 63, 105, 125
thought, 21, 35, 62, 97, 102, 127
Tim Berners-Lee, 14
time, 12, 20, 77, 121, 139, 143
today, 44, 68, 135, 139
tool, 14, 29, 44, 90, 105
tracking, 26
traction, 42–45, 103, 138
training, 4, 37, 52, 54, 116
transformation, 24
transparency, 5, 21, 23, 30, 35, 44, 54, 64, 68, 79, 95, 116, 121, 127, 129, 131, 140
trend, 135
trust, 5, 29, 35, 44, 54, 64, 66, 68, 77, 96, 97, 108, 121, 136, 140

uncertainty, 40
understanding, 3, 9–11, 13, 15, 20, 24, 26, 30, 45, 114, 138, 140
unemployment, 60
university, 20
upbringing, 12
uplift, 11

*Index*

usability, 26
usage, 20, 89, 139
use, 4, 5, 31, 59, 63, 90, 116, 129, 141
user, 5, 6, 10, 11, 14, 21, 22, 26, 33–35, 41–45, 54, 61, 62, 64–66, 68, 72, 73, 77, 96, 97, 101, 103, 108, 110, 114, 115, 121, 127, 129, 137, 138, 140, 144
utilitarianism, 11
utility, 4

validation, 41, 73
value, 10, 41–43, 45, 115
variety, 114
venture, 66
visibility, 44, 62
vision, 12–14, 21, 26, 33, 37, 40, 41, 48, 50, 89, 97, 109, 128, 131, 143, 145
voice, 62, 95, 97, 116

waste, 129, 130
water, 87, 125
wave, 99
way, 7, 13, 26, 31, 42, 57, 63, 83, 92, 95, 104, 108, 112, 114, 116, 131

wealth, 90, 92
web, 14
welfare, 144
well, 3, 4, 6, 7, 11, 21, 23–26, 30, 33, 42, 43, 45–47, 50, 53, 58, 61–63, 65, 68, 72, 73, 77, 85, 108, 109, 112, 114–116, 131, 136, 137, 139, 141, 143
whole, 90, 131, 141
work, 3, 13, 14, 23, 24, 30, 31, 36, 37, 74, 75, 90, 99, 102–104, 115, 128, 130, 131, 138, 141
workplace, 21, 124
workshop, 30
world, 5, 9, 14, 17, 18, 50, 58, 73, 90, 92, 109, 125–129, 133, 135, 137
worth, 138

Yamamoto, 6, 7, 27–29, 38, 61–63, 66, 70, 77, 79, 90, 92, 97–99, 101, 102, 116, 124, 125, 137–139
year, 20
youth, 94

Milton Keynes UK
Ingram Content Group UK Ltd.
UKHW021043111124
451035UK00017B/1371